EVERYTHING OUT OF CONTROL

Dorrie Buller

ISIS
LARGE PRINT
Oxford

First published in Great Britain 2003
by Isis Publishing Ltd.

Published in Large Print 2003 by ISIS Publishing Ltd,
7 Centremead, Osney Mead, Oxford OX2 0ES
by arrangement with Dorothy F. W. Robinson

British Library Cataloguing in Publication Data
Buller, Dorrie
   Everything out of control. – Large print ed.
   – (Isis reminiscence series)
   1. Buller, Dorrie
   2. Large type books
   3. Northamptonshire (England) – Biography
   I. Title
   942.5'5082'092

ISBN 0–7531–9928–9 (hb)
ISBN 0–7531–9929–7 (pb)

Printed and bound by Antony Rowe, Chippenham

EVERYTHING OUT OF CONTROL

CHAPTER
ONE

I was perched on the back stairs when disaster struck! It had always been a nice safe place to sit. With the door leading into the kitchen firmly closed. I must say I had listened to quite a few conversations, but not one had been as dreadful as this. We were moving, and at the age of seven this was nothing short of tragedy. I was leaving all my friends and everything I knew. It seemed as if life would never be the same again.

My short life had been spent in this Northamptonshire village, in an old farmhouse which overlooked the Top Green — for there were two greens. The lower one was where the school I had attended from the age of five was situated. The school was a long building with three classrooms. An avenue of limes stood sentinel between the green and the school. On Autumn days we children shuffled our feet with lovely "swishing" sounds through the fallen leaves and we brushed them with twigs to outline our imaginary houses — what mansions we planned!

Halfway between school and home was my favourite shop — one of three in the village. It was here, with my Saturday penny, I would stand making up my mind as I gazed in at the small cottage window before entering the shop, which was arrayed with sherbet dabs, liquorice and four humbugs for a penny (old money). It took quite a lot of thinking over.

Then there were Sundays; Aunt and I . . . but I had better explain: — I lived with my Grandmother, Aunt Flo and my Father, for sadly my Mother had died, aged 24, when I was just eight days old. But as I was saying — Aunt and I walked across the Top Green, carrying our Sunday dinner. We were taking it to the Bake House to be cooked in the large bread ovens, along with many more from the Village.

Then, of course, being Sunday, there was Sunday School to attend at the Baptist Chapel and later on the "Grown-Up" Service. We sat at Harvest Festival beneath jam jars suspended from the hat pegs, which lined the walls. The jars were precariously filled with flowers and suspended above the heads of the unsuspecting congregation!

But now there would be no more rides with my Father, in the milk cart, with its rattling churns, as Tommy the old black pony trotted at a fair pace to the railway station each morning, and worse still there would be no more penny bars of chocolate bought from the slot machine on the station platform, which were eaten with relish on the way home.

I wondered who would live in our old house and if they would whitewash the walls of the old barn and garland it with sprays from the hedgerows, as we had done, for the Sunday-school treat. In the barn the tea was laid out on long trestle tables, with yellow slab cake and fish paste sandwiches, then later on there would be

2

sports in our field and best of all sweets would be given as prizes!

Even worse — I would miss the swing boats on the village green at the local annual fair. Then there was the cattle market, held fortnightly behind the Red Lion Inn, when plenty of activity took place in the village.

So many memories flooded back and I wished — Oh! how I wished I had not sat on the back stairs that day! I did not want to leave all this and so much more.

The dreaded day came all too quickly when my Father and a boy herded our cattle together and set off with Tommy pulling the float, walking and riding, part of the way to our new home. I suppose it was fifteen miles or so away, in another county, but to me it seemed a far-distant place.

At the end of that day, the cattle were left for the night in a farmer's field and my Father and his helper rode home, only to begin again the next morning. The cows were milked and the milk left in payment for the use of the field. Then the slow business of walking and riding began again.

At last the new farm was reached and the animals were safely penned in the farmyard. Thankfully my Father and the boy made their way along the winding street to the Village Inn, where the kind landlady gave them newspapers to pad their legs — their trousers were so wet for it had been raining all day. After a meal of bacon and eggs, which she cooked for them, they retraced their steps to the farm. By this time we had arrived! I cannot remember what transport we had, but there we were and the furniture as well.

I can see it so clearly still — Dad walking down the village street, which didn't look anything like the one we had left, but he had a lovely collie dog with him, bought for 1/6d with its collar and chain thrown in! We named him Tib.

CHAPTER TWO

The house was old and although I did not know it then, I now know that I grew to love it as I have loved no other. So many years have gone since those days, but I think of it still. The house stood well back from the road, partially surrounded by farm buildings, and on the March Lady Day of 1927 we entered through the front door, which was almost like a church door in size, with carvings of Tudor roses around it. The wall by the door had iron rings fixed in it, to tie the horses to in days gone by.

The hall floor was old blue flag stones; one had a curious iron ring in it. We then came to the sitting room with its vast inglenook and a cold uninviting range. Each side of the range were seats, with small cupboards above (no doubt these were where the salt used to be kept), and beneath the seats were yet more spaces — perhaps to store wood and sticks with which to light the fire.

The kitchen led from the sitting room. It had a brown sink and one cold water tap. Across the hall, the drawing room with sash windows which overlooked the garden, and away to the left a long passage and winding stairs to the four bedrooms and long landing above.

Then yet more stairs to the attics, into which, in the 10 years we were there, I never ventured.

The garden was lovely, with high, flat-topped stone walls. Fruit trees and filbert nuts grew there as well as old-fashioned roses and lilacs, guelder rose and sweet-scented orange blossom. We discovered these as the seasons came and went. They were all bushes that had been allowed to grow to vast heights. Between the lawns, ancient yew trees grew. They formed an arch which is where Dad fixed a swing for me later on. There was variegated holly and a huge cherry tree, which every year had so much blossom, but sadly no fruit; however, it was a thing of beauty, so white and so pure and, against the blue sky, so very lovely. Four large vegetable areas were divided by paths, and in the distance, at the end of this long and beautiful garden, there was a little white gate. This led to the paddock past two low walls at the end of the garden; these did not detract from the view past the ha-has, which divided the field from the garden.

In the paddock a small stream gurgled on its way. It ran from the village pond beside a small pathway the other side of the garden wall, where it joined our field and made its way to our next one and then on to I knew not where — because that was the end of our boundary.

Adjoining the house were two buildings — one the top kitchen, with its two coppers, one of them so high and the other suitable for laundry. The bottom kitchen had at some time been a house or part of a house; there was a fireplace in it and two rooms. In one, our hens nested and perched on the roughly made ladder which led to the upstairs room. In the far end our fuel was kept, and doors led to the farmyard and again into the garden.

Japanese anemones and old crimson phlox grew in a small bed outside, and on the wall a vine flourished producing small purple grapes. They were very sour. Another gate led to the orchard, which was a sheer delight. Apples, pears and plums, also a morello cherry grew in abundance, and at the end a lovely walnut tree grew. I discovered if I climbed onto the wall, for here again stone walls surrounded orchard and paddock, I could perch on a branch and survey the village, while swinging gently to and fro. The old tree creaked and groaned, but it did not let me dowel.

The village was on a hillside, small rows of stone cottages faced down towards the pond and village green. Under one of the cottages a small spring, with a stone trough, in which a shamrock grew made a pretty feature. The Chapel was on top of the hill and on the hillside lilacs and laburnum bloomed from some long forgotten garden and in the Autumn crab apples lay in the mud on the roadside.

Again, as at my previous village, I attended Chapel, dressed in my best clothes. There were times when I missed Chapel, because by this time I had made a friend and we had hit on the brilliant idea of reading the Bible to an old gentleman in the village. He lived in one of the cottages, and each Sunday my Grandmother sent him a warm dinner. I can see it now, the roast beef, which had been cooked in the kitchen range oven, (for there was no bake-house, as in the previous village.) cut so thinly, and on the tin dish the gravy brown and thick, flavoured with the juices from the meat, was poured over the beef and vegetables. The slice of Yorkshire pudding — it was from a large tin cooked under the meat which was balanced on a stand, so the meat had dripped all its richness into it. So a generous slice of this delicacy balanced on top of the meat and vegetables, fresh from our own garden — then the whole was covered with a lid to keep it warm. Off I then trotted up the village street, where the old gentleman, with his bone handled knife and fork on a tin tray, let me into his sparsely furnished room.

The front door led into this small stone-flagged room, with its deal table and a couple of hard chairs and one wooden armchair, the latter in front of the small range. A rag rug lay in front of the hearth — that was the only degree of comfort. During the week we collected the dish in readiness for the next Sunday.

Sunday was a really special day, for all through the long summer evenings, Dad, Tib and I walked through the well loved fields to the top field and beyond, to a foot-path, through a neighbour's fields to what was in those days called the Turn Pike, and so home along the road to supper and bed. Up the narrow winding stairs — no candle needed for it was Summer, and we were all in our feather beds before ten o'clock.

I loved these walks, we always kept to the footpaths, but as I walked through the fields with the golden corn, poppies and scabious, the corn was almost as tall as I was, and as I ran my hand along the ripe ears I could

8

hear the lovely swishing sounds it made. Sometimes we forsook our fields and walked to the top of the village to Mill Road — a quiet country lane, as indeed they all were in those days, only an occasional bicycle could be seen and maybe a horse and trap. At the top of Mill Road the fields led to what may have been the site of an old mill — here a winding stream meandered peacefully along. I could jump and hop, without getting my feet wet, first from one side of the stream and then to the other.

Come Monday, work on the farm continued and Joe, who helped my Father, walked from his village two to three miles away, to begin the long day's work. At the end of the day, tired, but accepting it as his lot, he would walk the two to three miles home. The same procedure was carried out by Mary, who helped my Gran and Aunt with the housework. Mary lived in another village two miles away. All for a few shillings a week, winter and summer, whatever the weather.

In the summer an elderly (or so he looked) Irishman appeared. He slept in the barn and helped out on the land. Where he came from and where he went to we never knew, but he had traced us from the previous farm.

At one stage Dad thought he would have a lad to live in and help out on the farm, so after making enquiries, he engaged Tom from a near-by village. Tom was to share our table and fireside. Dad harnessed up the pony and set off the fourteen miles or so, to collect the new helper. I felt quite excited and pleased we were going to have someone new in our midst! At teatime Dad and

Tom arrived — Tom didn't say much as we sat down to tea. He hung his head and looked miserable. I thought it was about time I got him to talk! Passing the bread and butter hadn't done much good, he didn't seem very interested in his food.

"Don't be afraid if you hear a noise when you go to bed." I said kindly, "it will only be the rats in the house." I don't know what possessed me to say that! We had never had rats indoors. But it certainly broke the ice — Tom burst into tears and said he wanted to go home! That was it! I wasn't exactly popular — Dad had to drive him all the way home and the poor pony got more than its fair share of exercise that day. This finished the thought of anyone living in!

CHAPTER
THREE

The seasons came and went, bringing the work they entailed

I always loved the Spring. It would soon be with us and by this time the lambs would be in the fields. A few had put in an early appearance; these were housed behind bales of hay and straw and were made cosy and warm in the barns. Some were brought up on the bottle and there were many cold dark evenings, when the hurricane lamp was lit and we wended our way in the darkness to feed the orphaned lambs with bottles of warm milk and water. In the Spring, although the bottle-fed lambs were in the fields with the others, they were always tame and ran to meet us. We started the lambs off in the paddock, but even as close to the house as that, it didn't deter the fox. Stealthily at night he would stalk his prey; if it wasn't the lambs, he would try to get into the hens and ducks where he would cause havoc.

With Spring the primroses would be in bloom. They grew on the banks of our little stream, which flowed from the paddock into the leg o' mutton field, so named, I suspect, because of its shape. Violets also grew there, wild gooseberries and willows abounded. Every

Easter I put on my Wellington boots and waded into the stream to fill my small basket with flowers to take to the village Church, to decorate for Easter. Then with lovely fresh green moss, which we found in part of the Churchyard, I helped to fill the small glass jars with the flowers, standing them in beds of moss around the pillars of the Church.

The leg o' mutton field had a secret place. I stood in awe, clutching my Father's hand, as I gazed at the large stone where the devil was supposed to sit at midnight! This was a large flat stone which jutted from a cave-like place where no grass or plants grew — there was just bare earth and everything seemed silent, no birds nested or sang in the overhanging trees. Further in the field were gorse bushes, which formed a lovely low place. Had it not been so prickly it would have made a wonderful hiding place.

It was years later that I made up a story about a hedgehog who lived under the gorse igloo and kept a hat shop. The hats were made from wild flowers and leaves and pinned with thorns! That was for the pleasure of my daughter and later on my grandchildren.

Always there would be a few gorse flowers in bloom. Then we had a beautiful long hedge in the leg o' mutton field, under which large dog violets grew. It was a hawthorn hedge with tender green shoots of "Bread and Cheese" which were nice to eat. The poor little lambs, as they grew, had their tails taken off. These were a delicacy! Aunt and Gran stood for what seemed like hours, plucking the wool from the tails, which were then immersed in steaming hot water. When clean of wool, the long anaemic strips of tails were laid in rows in a baking tin and baked in the oven. Would we even bother or fancy them today? The great iron saucepans simmered the vegetables on the hob and our sitting room was a warm and welcoming place as dinner cooked.

CHAPTER
FOUR

However, in the Summer, the old range stood empty and cold. A three-burner paraffin stove, with a tin oven on top, was used instead and the sitting room was cool and pleasant. There were two windows, one overlooked the farmyard and the other the garden, where Gloire de Dijon roses nodded their heads and white jasmine climbed sweetly around Gran's bedroom window.

Rising early in the morning I always knew if it was going to be a hot day as I watered Gran's pot plants, so many of them placed around the front door — agapanthus lilies, fuchsias, huge red cacti and many others — for now it was Summer and the hay-making was in progress. The fields which had been shut up for the Spring, now with luck dependent on the seasons would show promise of a good crop. The mown grass was raked into long rows, turned and dried in the sun and the put into haycocks. The patient horses stood between the shafts of the wagon. At times they flicked their tails and tossed their heads as flies bothered them. We gathered alder sprays and placed it in the harness to keep the flies off. The hay was loaded onto the wagon, one man on top and another one pitch forking the hay up to him, to pack evenly, then it was taken to the rick,

14

this time to unload, as the old horse waited patiently. The hay was unloaded and the building of the rick took place. The ride back to the field in the empty wagon was eagerly awaited by us children, for invariably there would be quite a few of us, but all too soon it was over and we would amuse ourselves by making nests in the hay, until the next load was emptied.

Tea in the hayfield was always a delight — Aunt Flo arrived with cans of tea, home-made cakes and either jam or paste sandwiches, or sometimes a fresh cos lettuce or a bunch of radishes and even mustard and cress grown in our garden, washed and fresh. There was always a screw of salt to go with it. We children kept a bottle of lemonade in the shade from the trees. The lemonade was made from powder bought from the village shop, diluted with water.

The only shop was situated in the middle lane in the village. The lane was a steep unmade road, and to get to the shop we passed an old orchard, where in their season, bright rosy red apples grew. Pausing to admire, I would see, in the distance, our fields with the recently built hayricks. Soon the ricks would be thatched to keep out the rain. And I could see, nestling in the fold of the hills on the edge of the village, our house and the barns, the pond on the green, where Aunt Flo's Aylesbury ducks swam and dived for the small fish. We, as children, tied string around the top of jam jars and pulled them through the water, hoping to catch tadpoles and minnows.

The shop sold many things — groceries, sweets, paraffin and candles, vinegar sold from the barrel, reels of cotton, to name but a few items. At the end of the shop there was a Post Office and in a little booth in the adjoining shed was the telephone. Probably the only one in the village!

Further up the lane were one or two cottages. This was where the road divided into two ways, one towards the Church and the other towards the Methodist Chapel, but directly in front was the school — a small building with just one classroom which had a tortoise stove in the centre. The school was attended by twenty or so children.

Although it was Summer, holidays at the seaside were non-existent, but my maternal Grandparents lived in a small hamlet of eight houses back in Northamptonshire. Since retirement from their farm, they had a small-holding where they kept goats, chickens and a faithful old dog. I enjoyed going there to stay, although the first night away from home I was always sick with excitement! Gran and Grandad must have enjoyed my visit, for the first night I sat up in bed, between them, feeling sick and no sleep was had by any of us that night! They were good and patient though when I was small.

Then there was the trip to Northampton in the bus, that was the high-light of the week. I was wearing my best silk stockings having arrived at the age of twelve, oh! and my fancy garters were quite the thing! I had a blue pair and a pink pair both adorned with blue and pink rosebuds. My pocket was full of money, but not for long. I had no sooner got to Northampton when I tripped on a tram line, spilt my money and cut a large hole in the knee of my lovely stockings! One way and another it was a disastrous day — Gran bought a bottle of ammonia and a pork pie and on the way home the ammonia leaked all over the pork pie. Gran, however, was a great one to laugh at her misfortunes.

My Grandfather drove a pony and small trap so we usually had several rides out. One was to buy groceries three miles away, in a small railway town which had a sprinkling of shops. To get there we had to go up several steep hills — Grandad walked beside the pony while Gran and I rode in the trap. If the day was wet we sheltered under a big gig umbrella while Grandad and the pony got wet!

In the evening the gramophone was brought out, a large trumpet contraption, and sounds of "The Laughing Policeman" issued forth, or Grandad would play his violin and make up songs — short verses, usually about me!

Another treat was the greenhouse with lots of tiny sun warmed tomatoes. Gran baked tarts, scones and cheesecakes, which were placed on large meat dishes and left on the parlour table. These were a treat too.

The garden had dwarf fruit trees, rambler roses and gladioli, with a frame of double violets. The gladioli were planted along a border and a narrow path, along which Gran accompanied me on dark nights, to the three seater small house, with its squares of newspaper suspended from a loop of string. No mod cons in those days. There was also a mile of laurel hedge to be clipped by hand. It was a lovely place to stay, but all to soon it was time to go home, the holiday was over. The trip home had to be on a Thursday, when buses ran to Banbury market.

Gran and I reached Banbury, after having been around several small villages en route, so it had taken some time to get there. In the market square, where the poultry and eggs were being auctioned, what a noise there was to be sure. The market held so many interesting stalls and best of all there was a café, where my Grandmother always went for lunch. They knew her well and greeted her like an old friend. She ordered a ham roll and a lemonade for me — it was quite my favourite food! Gran then handed me over to my Father, who had been to the cattle market. Soon we were on our bus going home to my other Gran, Aunt Flo and Tib.

CHAPTER
FIVE

It was so good to be home again. One of our eight cats had had kittens on top of the high copper whilst I was away, only bringing them down when their eyes were open. The crafty cat knew it was too late to dispose of them, so they played on the lawn, all four of them in and out of an upturned shopping basket.

I enjoyed riding my bicycle again. This was a small machine with only a back brake. Although I had not had it very long, I was becoming quite proficient, or so I thought! I could ride with just one hand on the handle-bars and all sorts of things, but the day came when I excelled myself. I was riding along the road when I saw two people, the man was on a bicycle, riding slowly by a lady, who was walking — he had his hand on her shoulder. The front wheel of his bike steered out a little and then in a little and I did not know what to do — I had to pass them, but I had not come across anything like this before, so bearing in mind I had always been told to keep to the side of the road, I shot between them, knocking him off his bike! I don't know who was the most surprised out of the three of us.

Before Summer finally ended elderflower and dandelions were gathered in readiness for wine making. The flowers would be laid in large trays to dry in the sun. The elderflowers were shaken from the heads we had gathered and the dandelion petals would be plucked from their stems. Wine making was one of Gran's pastimes and in the top kitchen huge containers of liquid, with yeast floating on bits of toast were always in the process of fermenting. The slightly sour smell of this did not tempt me but the blackberry — well, that was lovely sweet and syrupy, and if I was lucky I was allowed to sip from my Father's glass.

Every evening, when he sat by the fireside, in his big green velvet chair with Tib by his side, Gran would bring in a large glass of home made wine for him. If it was winter she brought in a saucepan as well and the elderberry wine would be heated up over the glowing coals. It was good to keep out the cold at that time of year. Aunt Flo wrinkled her nose — she was strictly TT having signed the pledge!

CHAPTER
SIX

Autumn brought the fruit gathering. The plums and cherries had long since been gathered and made into jam or bottled in readiness for the long winter months, but now the apples glowed red on the trees and were ready for picking. There were so many varieties, some that would keep and some that would not, so they had to be gathered separately. There were two early varieties (unknown to me), but so sweet and juicy, as soon as they were ripe I stood and ate my fill.

Further in the orchard were the Blenheims, codlings and bramley seedlings, northern greens, pippins and many others, and one lovely yellow apple we called sugar and cream. Clothes baskets were filled to overflowing and were carried down the steep bank of the orchard, through the little gate into the garden and so to the top kitchen, where large salting leads were ready for the fruit to be laid out and stored.

Apple picking coincided with Banbury Fair. The third Thursday in October saw the streets of Banbury and the market place filled with wooden horses, ghost trains and much more. On the Thursday morning I was impatient to go, but first I had to go to the Dairy Show with Dad, because unfortunately for me, it fell on the same day, but by lunchtime I was able to go to the fair! I rode on the wooden horses and went on the small roundabouts. We saw the bearded lady and bought Banbury cakes and brandy snaps to take home as a "Fairing" for those who had not been so fortunate as I to go to the fair.

Thursday was always market day for Dad — he wore his best cord breeches and brown (well polished) boots and leggings, together with his best trilby hat and he always carried a cane. He was tall (over six foot), an upright man with a friendly manner and kind blue eyes. I am sure he enjoyed his day out, meeting other farmers and doing a little shopping for Gran. His return from Banbury, after visiting the Maypole grocers for cheeses and cream crackers, was something I greedily awaited and then of course there was *Tiger Tim* or *Rainbow* to read. He always bought me a comic on Thursdays.

The carrier also came. He would come on a Wednesday evening to collect our order and on Thursday morning he would set off for Banbury in a large hooded cart pulled by an old horse. He had collected his lists of errands from most of the village. Sometimes it was nightfall before he returned. Most households would be waiting for him, ready with a cup of tea and ripe for a gossip when he called.

I didn't like Mondays very much. This was washday, which entailed the disruption of Monday dinner. Washday was an operation in itself for early in the morning a woman from the village arrived, ready for a full day's work. The washing was done in the top kitchen. One of the coppers had a fire beneath it, and the water had to be carried in buckets from the cold tap in the kitchen, through the sitting room, along the hall, up a step into the garden, along about 30 feet of garden path and up another step, and then finally poured into the copper.

The clothes were boiled, rinsed and blued, then wrung by being mangled between giant rollers while some one turned the great iron handle. They were then ready to be pegged on the lines in the garden to dry. The copper was emptied and the water was used for scrubbing the toilet seats — two of them, side by side in a little house, tucked away past the top kitchen along a little path. Deal-topped tables and floors were also scrubbed, while dinner consisted of cold meat, pickles and left-over vegetables warmed up!

Tuesday was devoted to ironing. The large flat irons were heated on a trivet on the range in winter, or on a Valour stove in the Summer. The irons were spat on to see if they were the right temperature. It must have required patience, for nine times out of ten the irons blacked the clothes.

Before Winter there was great excitement in the village. Evangelists pitched their tent in my friend's field and proclaimed all would be welcome at their meetings. We children could hardly wait for the appointed time. There, in the large tent, chairs were placed on the grass in rows. On the platform there was a small piano, which was placed at the edge of the dais and a chair was on the grass near by. These were to enable the preacher's wife to accompany the rousing choruses. We are H.A.P.P.Y., we sang with gusto. Then it happened. Whether the pianist drummed too heavily on the keys, or whatever went wrong, the piano collapsed on top of her! The preacher leapt to the rescue and we were indeed H.A.P.P.Y.! It was a most enjoyable evening.

Before the evening was over, the preacher announced there would be a competition. We had all been issued with chorus books and we were asked to cover them nicely — the best would receive a prize! Well, I wondered what I could cover mine with and eventually came up with the idea of left-over wallpaper. My bedroom had lovely paper on the walls, sprays of pink apple blossom with little birds of blue perched on the branches. It looked very pretty, but it didn't win the prize.

November brought more excitement. I had been to the village shop and bought sparklers and a Catherine wheel, also a rocket or two. When darkness fell, Dad, Aunt Flo and I, with the aid of a hurricane lantern, made our way down the long garden path to the low flat walls at the end of the garden. Gran promised to watch from the window. Standing well back we watched Dad light the fireworks, greatly daring I held a sparkler in my hand. How pretty they were, but soon it was all over and time for bed. Another November the 5th gone.

A wonderful thing happened one year — we had our first wireless set. It was a crystal set with headphones.

We all had to sit very quiet and not even rustle a paper. The person with the headphones sat with rapt wonderment on their face, as they listened to a world outside the farm. Life was progressing.

CHAPTER
SEVEN

Winter days brought snow and ice. Dad and Joe would take a large hay-knife and cut into the ricks of hay to feed the cattle; in the barn we would grind Swedes and mangolds to mix with the cow cake. The fodder was carried shoulder high, in large milk pans, to fill the mangers for the cows when they came in to be milked. The snow lay in an unbroken carpet of white in paddock and orchard, save for the footprints of fox and birds. Taking my sledge I would drag it to the top of the paddock hill and then, sheer bliss, slide all the way down.

There is no magic compared with the Christmases of my childhood. My stocking was hung in the inglenook, for I wasn't brave enough to allow Father Christmas to come into my bedroom. I generously left him a mince pie and a cup of cocoa, and equally generously he left me a Blenheim apple, an orange, pink and white sugar mice and a penny in the toe of my stocking.

For days I had laboriously fashioned paper chains out of strips of coloured paper, bought from the village shop, and flour and water paste that Aunt Flo had mixed for me. These works of art would be hung across the sitting room. On the maroon plush overmantel which graced the inglenook, sprays of holly were artistically pinned by Aunt Flo. Our garden walls were ideal places for large leaved ivy to grow, and this with laurel and lovely variegated holly, from our tall tree, made the sitting room a very festive place.

Gran would produce a dish of walnuts and Blenheim apples, saved especially for Christmas. Aunt Flo made the most luscious flaky pastry mince-pies and cheese cakes and these, with the home-made raised pork pie, were something special to look forward to. The pie was for breakfast on Christmas morning. For dinner (mid-day — we always called it dinner) we would have one of the large cockerels from the farmyard, followed by homemade Christmas pudding. There were crackers too!

Sometimes carol singers came to our front door — usually children satisfied with a copper or two.

This was a happy time which continued for 10 wonderful years, but gradually things changed. For six months my dear Dad lay in his half-tester bed, in the room where from the windows he could see his beloved cows grazing peacefully on the hillside. That last Christmas we laid the table in his bedroom and carried the dinner upstairs to share with him — no-one wanted much and by February 1937 he had succumbed to the dreaded tuberculosis. At the age of 47 he had passed away. Gran was ill as well, with another incurable complaint. We didn't know who would leave Aunt Flo and me first but it was Dad.

So the day of the farm sale came, cattle, implements and some of the furniture was auctioned. That

September we moved Gran by ambulance and Aunt Flo and I closed the door of the dear old home for the last time.

Dad was dead, Tib had gone to a neighbouring farm and we, with one of the cats, were going to a near-by village to a cottage.

CHAPTER
EIGHT

How strange it seemed: generations of my paternal ancestors had lived in the village we were going to, indeed Gran, Aunt and my Father had left the family home there to go to a smaller farm in Northamptonshire, when my Grandfather, Dad's Father, had died. It was always understood that when Gran had become a widow, she had said she would never return to see someone else in her old home. Now she was returning, by ambulance and not to the farmhouse she had lived in, to the same village, full of memories of her early life as a young wife and mother — soon after to be laid to rest in the family burial plot, in that peaceful Churchyard with her husband and son, and her daughter Clarrie, who had also died of TB at the age of 20.

Then there was just Aunt Flo and I (at the age of 17) with not much money and a sadly depleted family.

The cottage was stone, double fronted, the end one of four, and awful as it sounds, I could not get used to the long garden which stretched alongside others. Eventually the cottage became home in a sense, and the house for over 40 years was kind to me. There were three bedrooms, two downstairs rooms and a small lean-to kitchen. From the outside the house was deceptive, but inside the rooms, with the exception of the kitchen, were spacious. A garage stood at the side of the house and a back gate with "Beware of the Dog" on it led into the garden, a stone barn and another garden beyond. A large Bramley apple tree and a couple of plum trees were all the fruit trees there were — not a lot after the orchard and garden we had left, but at least it was something and in fact the apple tree yielded bumper crops for many years.

It was time to begin work, for the short time after leaving school I had stayed on the farm, which, if things had been different would have been my life, I suppose. School I didn't enjoy. At the age of 11, I had gone daily to Banbury on the bus, to a private school. However I was now 17 years of age, not fitted for much, so for a short time I attended a school for typewriting and shorthand. My first job was in an office as a junior filing clerk, so the typing and shorthand were not much needed. Then I left and took on an insurance round, walking in town and cycling in the countryside to collect premiums. This was an education in itself, learning to arrive as soon as possible after the pay packet in some cases.

Aunt Flo, to augment her income, took in a "paying guest" and later on she decided to open a small sweet shop. There were no shops in the village. She bought a few sweets, put up a card table in the porch and was ready for business. Later (maybe the weather changed), she transferred her bottles and boxes to the cupboard under the stairs and put a few jars in the passage window. Her customers now came to the back door to be served. She didn't make much profit. Then war was declared and so everything was rationed. Sweets could only be bought with coupons, which involved more work, but she kept her little shop going.

Three families who had been evacuated from Coventry and London came to the village. We took in two mothers, three children and a dog — then at weekends a sister and all three husbands arrived. Where they all slept I do not know. Our next evacuees were a schoolmistress and her mother. Oh, and then there was a man on his own — dear Aunt Flo, trusting soul that she was, said he must be all right as he had brought his sugar ration with him! Although he didn't stay long, he was all right. Quite a few came and went, sometimes going home for the peace of the country was too much for them. We watched the glow in the sky over Coventry as it was bombed and felt so thankful to be safe in our village.

CHAPTER
NINE

I was now twenty-one years old and conscripted to factory work. Buses picked up the workers in the blackout and deposited them, including me, inside the factory gates. Special police inspected each identity card as we alighted from the buses. We then clocked in at the factory and day shifts took over from the night shifts — 6.00am to 2.00pm, 2.00pm to 10.00pm and 10.00pm to 6.00am. Work continued non-stop to help the war effort — music blared continuously. About 3.00am we made our way in the black-out to the canteen for early breakfast or call it what you will, for meals, and sleeping went haywire. A week on each shift didn't give your body time to adjust.

Hair was bundled up into a cabbage-net arrangement, which we called a snood, and daringly we wore trousers, mine being brown corduroy. All this to stop hair and skirts being tangled in the machinery.

After a few months I was transferred to the wages department on medical grounds, and I was solely on daytime hours. I had now time to enjoy the cinema, or go to country dances. Then I met Rob, a soldier in the Yorks and Lancaster Regiment, stationed quite near; six weeks we got to know each other and in that time I travelled to Yorkshire to meet his parents. Then he was sent overseas and for almost four years we wrote to each other every other day. How longed-for were those letters: I would meet the postman on the way to the office in the mornings, and he would pass over the airmail or aerographs (which were short letters photographed and reduced in size).

In the wages department, every few weeks, we stayed behind to pay out the ten o'clock shifts, then we were sent home in a staff car. I enjoyed my three years and a bit there. Then one day the phone in the office rang for me and Rob was home from India and Burma. We married by special licence before the week was out, and I obtained my release from war work to be with my husband.

It was a difficult time to think of a wedding on a large scale, and Aunt and I could not afford it anyway. With my clothing coupons I bought a sensible blue dress and jacket. A friend made a hat for me: it consisted of blue and maroon feathers and net. I carried a family prayer book of ivory and a spray of cyclamen was pinned to my jacket. I must say in the photograph they could have been mistaken for orchids! Everything went according to plan: all the guests had a drink (small) and a morsel of wedding cake and we received a lovely lot of presents — so I think we came off best!

It was difficult to find anywhere to stay in 1945 for our honeymoon, so arriving at Paddington we tried to find a hotel with vacancies that was within our means. Everywhere was full or too expensive and by seven o'clock that evening we took a train to Reading. That too seemed equally hopeless, so reviving our shattered nerves in the station refreshment room we confided our troubles to the lady serving behind the counter. She shook her head and vaguely suggested "maybe she could put me up for the night, if 'hubby' could find somewhere". This kind offer was declined with false thanks, especially by "hubby", who had braved the rigours of the Burma jungle only to come back to a frustrating situation like this.

Wearily we picked up our luggage and departed with strained smiles. Eventually we found a modest hotel and the week passed all too quickly.

Rob casually mentioned at breakfast one morning, that he had seen a sporty little car for sale at a garage down the road. I was delighted, never owning more than a bicycle in my entire life. I had visions of arriving home in style. The salesman was happy to take us for a trial run and so, trying to look as if buying a car was an every day occurrence, Rob wrote a cheque and we arranged to collect the car the following morning.

Now having transport we decided to spend our wedding present money. It would be so convenient to take things home "by car" — it would not matter how large and bulky the parcels were. "We will take it in the car." I said airily. It did sound grand, far better than "hang it on the handlebars" sounded!

We loaded our belongings into "Phoebe", for so we had fondly named this three-wheeled sporty little car, and then Rob, me and the parcels set off. We had hardly got out of the town when "Phoebe" made a funny noise, sputtered, and we came to an abrupt halt. Rob climbed out and lifted the bonnet and I sat ignoring the whole business, it was such a blow to my new found dignity! Finally Rob emerged from under the bonnet, not the nice clean Rob I knew, but grease-grimed and apologetic. "Perhaps you could give her a little push." he suggested. So there was I, my head down and my rear end gracefully arched, attempting to push a stubborn "Phoebe".

After a series of false starts something happened, the engine kicked over as if it really meant it. "Hurry." yelled Rob — we had made it and we settled down to enjoy the journey home, but not for long — "Phoebe" had to be coaxed, shoved and pushed. We eventually reached a garage and abandoned her to the tender mercies of a mechanic. We unloaded our parcels, suitcases etc., and wearily trudged to the nearest bus stop. So by bus and train we arrived home to Aunt.

CHAPTER
TEN

Much later Rob sold "Phoebe", or more or less gave her away, and in her place he bought a nice staid "soap-box". For a start it had four wheels, as I was right off anything with less. Fortunately it proved reliable, and some weeks later Rob, who had now been demobbed from the Army, felt it was time to look around and resume his long interrupted career once more. Eventually he was able to start a continuation of his pre-war work with estate agents. It was some distance away and would mean we had to move and find somewhere to live.

Easier said than done! After endless searching to no avail, we decided to load the car and go on the Sunday to search again for somewhere to live before Rob started work on the Monday. Sunday was a cold, but bright day and we arrived at the outskirts of the city at lunchtime. The car had behaved beautifully all the way — now however it did a "Phoebe" on us.

"I thought it was too good to be true." I said angrily, as I gazed through windows where families were sitting down to Sunday lunch. After what seemed an endless time the engine ticked sweetly over and we were again on our way. All the rest of that day we searched for somewhere to stay. Late that evening, desperate, we decided to go to an address that had refused us by letter when we applied for a flat. The woman took pity on us and said we could stay the night, but the flat was let from the following morning. Thankfully we carried our cases upstairs and climbed into bed.

Monday morning soon came and we again packed everything into the car and regretfully left the flat for the new tenants.

Rob drove to a car park near his office and then off he went to his new job, leaving me to take over the search for some sort of accommodation. It was hopeless — life just after the war was not easy! Rob met me at lunchtime but I had nothing to tell him; he did however speak favourably of his first morning at work.

At teatime we began a tour of the suburbs, stopping at each parade of shops to read the notice boards. On one of these a lady was advertising for "gentleman lodgers". Arriving at the council estate we knocked on the door of number 62.

"I don't take married couples." said the lady in question.

"What do we do now?" I asked, as we sat outside the house.

"There is not much alternative but to sleep in the car, if we can find somewhere to park it." replied Rob gloomily. We found the map and were just looking for some open countryside, when a voice at the window said, "Will you come inside again?" It was Mrs. McDonald!

It was agreed that Rob should stay there and I would return to Aunt's the following day, but for the night Mrs. McDonald would give up her bedroom to us. Miserably we parted in the morning, Rob to go to his office and me to the railway station and back home again. At least he could look for somewhere for us to live, so it was only a temporary set back.

The days passed slowly, I answered yet more advertisements and finally secured a job not far from Rob's employment. I also managed to get a bed at the YWCA in the city. When Rob came home at the weekend, joyfully I told him that on the Monday morning I would be returning with him. We could at least meet at lunchtime and spend the evenings together.

So there we were. Rob and I kissed good-night on the doorstep of the YWCA after yet another frustrating evening of searching for rooms. Then Mrs McDonald, who had invited me to tea once or twice, opened her heart and said that I could stay there until we found a flat, so life took a turn for the better and Mrs McDonald, bless her, looked after us like a mother.

At last we heard of some rooms. They consisted of a bedroom and sitting room and use of the kitchen and bathroom. The area was pleasant, the rooms well-furnished and, best of all, the rent was well within our means. We bade farewell to Mrs. McDonald and promised her we would keep in touch, for she had helped us over a difficult time and we were grateful.

So we moved to number six. Mrs Winter, the lady owner, was an elderly widow and disposed to be friendly. Her hair was iron grey, pulled back into a sparse bun, her blue eyes glinted through spectacles and she wore a somewhat ostentatious mourning brooch — complete with what I supposed was a lock of the late lamented Mr. Winter's hair!

I had arranged to work at the office on a part-time basis, finishing each day at lunchtime and returning to number six to do my household chores and cook a meal for Rob. Mrs. Winter was lonely, so she was waiting ready for a chat when I returned home, and invited me in to have a cup of tea with her in the afternoon. This became a ritual and went on for some time, then I began to feel unwell. The doctor prescribed that I rest in bed for a few days. I broke the news to Mrs Winter and tottered off to bed.

Shortly after that Mrs. Winter arrived in the bedroom and burrowed her bottom firmly into the flock mattress. She greeted me with "You are young to be like this." I assured her — apologetically — I was beginning to feel better. "A friend of mine had much the same thing as you, and she died!" Mrs Winter brought out the last word triumphantly! "The flowers were lovely, all over the floor they were."

"Really." I said feebly — having gone right off the small bunch of violets tastefully arranged in a paste pot by my bed. Much later, or so it seemed, Mrs. Winter took her departure. In a day or so I was fit and well again.

A neighbour mentioned two unfurnished rooms were to let on the other side of the town, which we had yet to explore. It would mean buying furniture and carrying meals up and down stairs, but we thought about it and decided to view. That evening we arrived at yet another estate. The identical semis greeted us and pink-frilled curtains adorned the front windows of the house, rather grandly named The Limes. There was not a lime tree to be seen: the best the occupiers could do was to plant a laburnum tree, under which two gnomes leered round a phoney toadstool.

The rooms were small, but in one there was a fireplace, with a small basket grate to hold the coals. We decided this would be our sitting room. We would have to give Mrs Winter a week's notice and we would need to buy some furniture, but it would be lovely to be able to use our own things at last.

On the way back to number six we discussed the best way of breaking the news to Mrs. Winter — in some ways our feelings were mixed, for it was far from pleasant to be elderly and alone. That weekend we told her, and sadly she didn't take it too well — but we had made our arrangements and there was no going back.

We decided to buy only the bare essentials. We ordered a bed, two bedroom chairs and a kitchen table. The delivery was promised for the following Saturday, which was when we hoped to move in. That weekend we packed our china, kitchen utensils, linen and clothes and bade farewell to Mrs. Winter.

Optimistically we went to our new home to find only two empty rooms with bare floorboards. "Never mind." said Rob, "The shop promised delivery, they are sure to come soon." We carried our things upstairs, we hung the curtains and waited. Eventually a van drew up —

the bed and mattress had arrived. These had been purchased from a different shop, and we felt fortunate the most essential things had arrived. I'd had visions of curling up for the night on bare boards!

On Saturday night we were still without the rest of our furniture — we sat disconsolately on our suitcases and viewed the array of clothing, now spread on newspapers on the floor. It was then we realised how inadequate our new home was. Money was far from plentiful and there seemed so many things we needed in order to live comfortably. The only thing to do, we decided, was to go to the weekly furniture auction on the Monday, to try to buy a wardrobe and cupboard. But first Sunday morning dawned. I tripped down to the kitchen to prepare our breakfast, carried it upstairs and placed it carefully on a hamper, which had to serve as our table. Then Rob and I squatted on the floor, one each side of the hamper! We ate every meal that day in the same way, and I must confess, my thoughts turned to our new landlord and his wife sitting in comfort downstairs.

On Monday morning the kitchen table and chairs arrived. The bedroom was already full with the bed! We erected the table in our sitting room, placed the two chairs either side of it, and sallied forth to the auction.

Rob and I looked around and marked various possibilities in our catalogue. One item that interested us was a white bedroom suite, which comprised of a large wardrobe, dressing chest, pedestal cupboard and tallboy. Rob went to the office leaving me to bid. We thought the bedroom suite would perhaps make too much money, but we were lucky — it was knocked down to me for £26.00.

When it arrived at the Limes we found that a great deal of manoeuvering had to be done, but at last we managed to squeeze the dressing chest into the bedroom. However the wardrobe, pedestal cupboard and tallboy had to stay in the sitting room. The furniture was not in its right setting but it did store all our belongings and that was all that mattered.

CHAPTER
ELEVEN

Life at the Limes was very different from that at Mrs. Winter's abode. During the day we went our separate ways. Vi, our property owner, was most easy to get along with and we didn't clash in the kitchen — unlike Mrs. Winter, who always seemed to have a milk pudding ready to pop into the oven when I was trying to cook our tea. Vincent, Vi's husband, was laying out the back garden. He worked hard, digging and planting. Soon a few flowers bloomed and in the vegetable plot early peas were ready for picking — Vi prepared them for their evening meal. "You know," she sighed, as she leaned gracefully against the kitchen door, "I wonder what I did wrong, those peas don't even look like the ones we get from the fish and chip shop — all nice and squashy."

We still went home to Aunt Flo's at the weekends, when petrol rationing allowed. No-one cared what time we arrived back, unlike Mrs. Winter, who had always kept a strict eye on the clock. Now, when the weather improved and the early mornings were light, we would get up at the crack of dawn to travel back to the city, just allowing enough time to get to the office.

The weeks and months passed. Rob and I often visited Mrs. McDonald, and her house was almost "home from home" for us. She always provided at least one of our favourite dishes at teatime. On one occasion she had prepared a lovely salad for us, as she knew I always enjoyed it. "I am sorry." I apologised, "I don't know why it is, but I seem to have gone off salad, and I'm afraid I can't drink tea these days. Now plums, they are something I long for." I said, warming to my subject. "It's funny but I buy a pound of them, and before I can get to the end of the road I have eaten them all." Mrs. McDonald smiled knowingly and suggested it might be as well if I had a check-up at the doctor's.

As I left the surgery, "Well?" asked Rob. My face was one huge smile.

"I'm pregnant and the baby is due in February!" We felt on top of the world. Although we had not planned on starting a family quite so soon, we were thrilled.

We continued living at The Limes, but it became increasingly difficult to cope with morning sickness and to carry meals up and down stairs. We knew we would have to move before long but where to?

I decided to give in my notice at the office. This was accepted with gloom. "Do you know," said my employer peevishly, "You are the third person to sit in that chair and become pregnant. There must be some kind of hog-do on it!"

Once I stopped working, the days seemed awfully long and dull. I missed the company of the others in the office a great deal, but in the mornings I had the kitchen to myself, and in the afternoon, a rest and a gentle walk to buy more plums!

Rob decided to think seriously about changing his job. He had seen one advertised in the local press. It was his kind of work and in the country and there was living accommodation as well! This was the deciding factor. It always seemed ironic that although Rob worked with estate agents, there was not one thing to rent.

Changing employment, especially as it was less money, needed a lot of thought. I knew he enjoyed his work with his present firm and that it was a good firm. We talked it over and decided, as Rob said, "There was no harm in applying". A few weeks later he was called for an interview in a small country town. It would be a far cry from the busy life of the city but so much more pleasant.

After what seemed an age, Rob returned from the interview, looking very pleased with himself. "I've got it and start in a months time!" The work was on a disused airfield, where families now resided in the Nissen huts. It was for Rob to get it all on a business-like footing, where the families paid rent and the huts were kept in good repair. It would take some organising and looking after and we were to live on the old airfield too — in the disused control tower!

The control tower would be ready for us to move in, in December.

"There will be two bedrooms a kitchen, living room and an office," said Rob, "And we can make a garden."

"We will have to buy some furniture." I said happily, because by this time I was feeling quite excited. It now seemed too good to be true, but I knew Rob was doing the right thing. The job prospects were excellent, and not only that, it would be sheer bliss to live in the country again.

We began to visit auction rooms again, and this time we bought a three-piece suite, which was upholstered in fawn and blue moquette. The springs were not very good, but we thought with a little work on it, it would be all right. A friend stored it until we were ready to move. Back at my Aunt's house we had several nice pieces of furniture which had belonged to my parents, and we knew these would help to fill the gaps in the spacious rooms.

At the day came to leave The Limes, the furniture van arrived early and we bade farewell to Vi and Vincent. We drove along following the furniture van. It was a cold November day and we had risen early to prepare for our departure, so we were more than ready to join the driver of the van at a transport cafe for hotdogs and cups of steaming coffee. Sometime in mid-afternoon we arrived at the disused airfield.

Children were playing on the heaps of rubble, and air-raid shelters and Nissen huts could be seen. Small gardens had been cultivated and "Mums" stood with arms folded as they watched the van and small car stop outside the control tower, which was situated a little distance from the Nissan huts.

We climbed the 14 steps to the brown front door. On opening it we were confronted with another 14 steps. I followed Rob upstairs, along a corridor and the door at the end opened into a room with large windows overlooking the vast spaces away across the airfield. A man was laying floors and whistling cheerfully.

"I understood the flat would be ready for us." Rob said. The whistling ceased.

"That's good one!" the man laughed, "It won't be ready for another fortnight, at least."

"Our furniture is downstairs." said Rob.

"You can stack it in the end bedroom, that's done. We've been held up for materials, so it's not possible to live here yet." the man said, with relish, I thought.

We realized we had no alternative, but to do as the man suggested, and then make our way to the hospitality of Aunt Flo's, which fortunately was only seven miles away.

The removal man was still waiting downstairs — Rob broke the news to him.

"28 steps," he said unhappily, "I suppose I better have a go."

Rob and he pulled, pushed and heaved the furniture, staggering up the stairs with it. Finally we had it all packed away in the bedroom and the furniture removal man left. I bet he never wanted to see a control tower again!

I viewed the rooms gloomily, concrete floors and large windows — the windows would be marvellous in Summer, but oh! how bitterly cold it was now. The wind whistled and howled and we were not sorry to close the door on it all. At least, we said thankfully we have a comfortable home to go to until the tower is ready so things could have been worse.

Fortunately Rob's work was within easy travelling distance, so that didn't present a problem. I caught up with visiting old friends, who looked aghast when I told them that we were going to live in the control tower. By mid December the flat was at last ready. It would be lovely to arrange our furniture and really establish a home of our own, for this felt like the real beginning for us as a family — our baby was due in mid February.

CHAPTER
TWELVE

It was a cold dark night when we finally came home to the Control Tower. Lights from the Nissan huts glimmered in the distance. All was quiet with the exception of the occasional bleat from the sheep on the airfield and the distant hum of traffic as it sped along the road. We put the key in our own front door — it was a nice feeling! The 14 steps loomed ahead of us, but at the top of them the rooms were waiting to be explored and they were all our own!

The door at the top of the stairs led into a large kitchen, the window of which faced the main road where we could see the beams from the car headlights and in which there was an oil stove for cooking. Leading from the kitchen was a small walk-in larder. It had a stone shelf and a little window, from which (in daylight) we could, from our lofty height, look down onto two disused toilet blocks and an air raid shelter. Next to the kitchen was a bedroom, fairly large, and this we decided would be our guest room. We wondered what we should furnish it with — Rob suggested yet another auction. Auctions! I was in no condition to go anywhere except the local maternity home! The office was a compact little room with a delightful view of the shed which would serve as a garage. At the end of the corridor was the sitting-room where the man had been laying floors. This room had two very large windows and a door that led to a balcony. A black coal range with an oven was provided for heating and cooking. It had a chimney pipe that disappeared out of sight. I could visualise the splendid meals I would cook, as childhood memories of kitchen ranges and good wholesome food flooded back. I felt confident that it would be simple to produce a home cooked hot meal — little did I know! I From the sitting-room another door led into another large bedroom which again had huge windows overlooking, what would one day be our garden. From these windows we could enjoy the view across the airfield.

Rob carried sticks and coal from the basement into the sitting-room and very soon he had managed to light a small fire. The range billowed smoke. "It's only natural," said the expert, "The pipe hasn't warmed up yet." We surveyed each other and our surrounding with streaming eyes. Gradually the fire settled down to a feeble but steady glow. We hung the curtains, which gave a degree of privacy — if only from the sheep! The curtains didn't quite meet, but they did look attractive against the cream walls. We could not afford carpets, but the brown lino we had bought had a tiled effect and we were lucky there was enough lino to lay a centre panel in the corridor. The surrounding floor we polished with a cheerful red polish.

Everything was beginning to take shape — it had been pleasant to huddle over our few embers for a brief rest and warm as we tried to visualise our room and the life we hoped to enjoy at the Tower.

"Large windows will give the baby lots of fresh air." I said.

"But have you thought of the problem of carrying a pram up and down 28 steps?" asked Rob.

However, nothing could dampen our enthusiasm, and it was with happy hearts and a feeling of well being that we closed the front door and made our way to the local inn to drink to our future.

Christmas passed and we made plans for moving. We had been to the Tower several times and had moved our furniture into place. The bedroom looked quite nice with the entire white bedroom suite in it, but the sitting-room was a bit bare. The settee we drew close to the range, the chairs were put each side of it. The table we placed under the window and that was all we had! Clearly another visit to an auction sale was imminent. Back at the cottage (my Aunt's home) we still had a bureau, a chest of drawers and a table. These we hoped to move as soon as possible for we needed quite a lot of furniture to make our new home comfortable. What had seemed to crowd small rooms at The Limes was absolutely lost in the spacious rooms of the Control Tower.

The day arrived when we moved to our new home — it was cold, but dry. Weak January sunshine shone through the windows. We soon got the fire going — again the smoke billowed forth. However, the range soon settled down and we were reasonably warm. As it was daylight, we opened the door onto the balcony and, after climbing yet more stairs, we arrived on the flat roof of the building. Strange as it may seem, someone at some time had erected a small shed which contained traces of it having been inhabited by chickens! It appeared almost impossible to think of anyone carrying chicken food and the chickens to that height. I wondered if they had clipped the chickens' wings to prevent them flying away — for they were a very long way from the ground.

The view from the roof was marvellous: acres of green fields, a giant patchwork quilt of countryside stretched before us. Slowly (I could do little else) we made our way down the iron stairway, through the sitting room, down the 28 steps and outside to the waste area. This ground was to be our garden. What lovely fresh vegetables and flowers we would grow!

The next morning, Rob got ready for work while I cooked breakfast on the oil stove. We enjoyed sitting at our table near the window, watching the occasional Land Rover drive along the runways.

CHAPTER
THIRTEEN

The days passed uneventfully. Often I did not speak to anyone all day, so I was glad to see Rob arrive home in the evening. The baby would soon be due, we were not on the telephone and the Maternity Home was 12 miles away. Towards the middle of February we decided the sensible thing would be for us to go and stay with my Aunt as she lived much nearer the hospital. For a short time we would have to bid goodbye to the Tower — it was a strange feeling to know, that if all went well, three of us would be returning.

A fortnight later our daughter was born, a tiny scrap weighing 5lbs 3oz. The day we took her home was sunny. We carefully wrapped our precious bundle in her shawl and carefully placed her in the carrycot before we made our way back to the Control Tower. It was good to be home again. On the airfield young lambs had made their appearance. The hedgerows were breaking into leaf and the bird song held a promise of Spring. For us life was perfect.

The Control Tower was not exactly warm. We made a glowing fire but the old range proved to be very frustrating — it depended such a lot on the direction the wind was blowing. Sometimes the oven was too fierce and at other times it absolutely refused to heat up at all. Cooking was a chancy business!

Fan, as we lovingly called her (her real name was Patricia, but she was Fan to us and still is to this day, so many years on), was a contented baby. In the mornings I placed her pram in front of the open windows and in the afternoon I struggled down the 28 steps, first with the pram and then a second time with Fan, who I had left safely in her cot while I made the first trip. I walked miles along the runways, stopping to gather buds from the hedgerows. Later in the year I picked Spring and Summer wild flowers. Very much later, as the months passed, Fan would sit up in the pram and joyfully try to grasp the flowers with her chubby hands.

One of the difficulties at the Control Tower was the water, or rather the lack of it. Sometimes our tap yielded only a trickle, for we were so high that there was not enough pressure to pump the water up to our lofty height. It was not easy to carry water from the rainwater tank, but there was no alternative! We did store some clean water in dustbins in the basement so I was able to do the laundry, which was then hung on the balcony to dry. This was an excellent drying ground, although rather precarious. Fan would lie happily in her pram by the window, watching the movement of the laundry as the wind whipped the clothes back and forth. As she grew older and could run around, I had to make sure she was safely in her playpen with enough to keep her occupied while I hung out the washing. Occasionally an extra strong gust of wind snatched some of the laundry from the line and would blow it across the airfield. As I rushed down the stairs and around the corner to try and catch whatever had blown away, I was always afraid that some disaster would strike. My worst fear was the door would slam shut and I would not be able to get to Fan.

We began to think of furnishing the other bedroom — first of all we needed a floor-covering. We also needed a floor-covering in the office for the cement floors puffed up clouds of dust.

Floor-covering can be costly, so Rob hit on the splendid idea of buying roofing felt and painting it with liquid lino. This was a great success — now that the floors were covered all we needed was furniture. The obvious thing was to arrange for the table, large bureau and chest of drawers to be moved from my Aunt's house to the Control Tower.

Rob made arrangements for a furniture van to deliver them — unfortunately it arrived at the Tower when Rob was out. To make matters worse the little man that delivered it was quite alone.

"I can't manage up all them stairs, missus, and that's a fact." he said.

It was frustrating having our lovely furniture so near, yet so inaccessible. I badly needed to fill up a few spaces in the large rooms.

"Can't deliver again this week," he removed his cap and scratched his head, "I thought there would be someone here to help me."

"Look," I said, "I'll help you carry it upstairs."

"It's pretty heavy, missus."

"Never mind," said I, all prepared to spring into action. "First of all we'll take the table!"

This was a crafty move on my part, as it was the lightest piece of furniture. We managed the table quite easily — I felt almost light-hearted as we made our way down stairs to collect the chest of drawers. Unfortunately it proved rather more difficult, but not deterred we staggered up and down. First with the drawers and then with the chest. It wasn't easy! The removal man shot the last drawer into place and stood back wiping the sweat from his brow.

"I'll make some coffee," I said, "before we tackle the last one." The removal man was not happy — I could tell from the way he spat on the paper as he rolled a cigarette. Somehow I felt entirely in sympathy with him — it just wasn't his day and thinking about it, mine neither!

Refreshed by the coffee and the brief rest, we returned yet again to the ground floor — this time for the bureau, a solid piece of furniture, fashioned by craftsmen of a by-gone age. With aching arms we carried the drawers upstairs, then, lifting the body of the bureau, I began to climb the stairs, backwards, the little man gallantly taking as much weight as he could. Poor little soul, I thought compassionately, as I gazed down over my end of the bureau at his flat cap. There he was bogged down with our furniture — looking absolutely exhausted! Supposing I dropped my end, I thought, I wonder what would happen?

Luckily no such thing happened, but where he found the energy to get down the stairs so quickly and leap into his van when the bureau was in place, I shall never know. I got the impression he could not get away fast enough! !

The Control Tower began to look furnished at long last. I stood back and admired the polished pieces of furniture as in the flickering firelight the table glowed and shone.

CHAPTER
FOURTEEN

Some weeks later Rob bought a double bed at an auction, and two tables — one for his office, the other one we could drape to use as a dressing table in the spare bedroom. Now we could invite visitors to stay. An invitation was speedily sent to our old friends, Peter and Carol. I had hoped that the weather would be warm and sunny for their arrival, so that the Control Tower would be at its most pleasant but this was not to be! The winds howled, from the outside the Control Tower looked bleak and uninviting, but indoors was as cosy as we could make it, which come to think of it, wasn't very cosy at all!

All night long the winds howled and buffeted around the Control Tower, Carol spent a very disturbed night, little pools of water were dripping from the walls, but we were used to this and the chilliness of the place did not effect us. We noticed our visitors appeared to be a bit cold, even though they were huddled close to the range, which had gone temperamental again due to the wind being in the wrong direction. The water pressure wasn't at it's best either.

"How the wind howls — doesn't it get on your nerves?" asked Carol. I just grinned and replied it could be sunny and peaceful sometimes. Explaining to Carol and Peter about the water pressure, or lack of it, and the cussidness of the range, I felt the visit was not going too well — but little did I know there was worse to come.

Later that morning I ventured onto the balcony to hang the washing on the clothesline Carol watched fascinated from one of the large windows. Then it happened! The wind got behind the door leading from the sitting-room to the balcony and almost whipped it from its hinges. This strained it so much that however much we tried, we couldn't close it. I gave up trying to hang the washing out — which had been a silly idea in the first place. Carol and I (the men were out) battled with the wretched door, but what with the force of the wind and the damage to the door, it was too much for even our combined strength to close it.

As a howling gale swept through the sitting-room, we leaned our weight against the door and wondered what we could do. The range, not to be out-done, started to billow smoke in all directions. It was obvious something had to be done, but what? Carol had a brilliant idea, tie the clothes-line to the door and fix the other end to the window, and this is what we did, just hoping that the window would not be the next thing to go. When our two respective husbands appeared, they found two exhausted females issuing orders for the door to be fixed before we eat.

The weekend had been a disaster. The Control Tower did not yet lend itself to visitors. We had adapted to our way of life, but as soon as we were thrown out of our routine chaos reigned.

Spring slipped away, and the days passed too quickly for us to do all the things we planned. The warm weather tempted us to begin our garden, so we began to clear the rough grass and weeds. This was hard work but wonderful exercise. We settled Fan in a sheltered spot and began to work. After a few hours we began to see results — the soil was now ready for digging.

We planted vegetables, salad ingredients (radish and lettuce) and herbs. We then made a long flower border, and in this we sowed antirrhinums and love-in-the-mist to name but two. Rob made a cold frame for more seed sowing.

It was satisfying and absorbing work making a garden, and from knowing that Fan would benefit from the fresh vegetables which could be pulped and strained. Looking back it was a miracle to me that we had any vegetables at all, but strangely the hares and rabbits, that we saw on the airfield left our garden well alone. I can only think that there was such an abundance of food for them that they did not have to search.

The warm sweet air wafted into our rooms. During the day we could not find a more pleasant place to sit than by the large open windows. We looked across at the long meadow grass waving in the breeze, and the corn which would soon be cut and stored to provide winter fodder for the cattle. The evenings and weekends were not so pleasant — lads on their motorcycles would arrive and roar around the runways for hours, making a deafening noise. Occasionally a small glider or aircraft would land — this caused great excitement among the children who lived on the airfield.

CHAPTER
FIFTEEN

Not many weeks passed without Rob going to another auction, so by this time we had acquired a plum coloured carpet (for the guest room), a bureau bookcase and a sideboard, three saucepans of various sizes with lids, and a copper kettle. The saucepans were quite black with verdigrease, but Rob had tentatively scratched the surface with his fingernail and discovered that underneath all the grime copper glinted. We cleaned them again and again until the saucepans were restored to their former splendour. One could imagine, in days gone by, the maids shining these kitchen utensils and choosing which ones to use, as they stood in front of the rows of shining pans hanging in the vast kitchens of "big houses". Each saucepan would be graduated in size and used to cook the rich sauces and vegetables for the master and mistress. We hung our pans over the range, while the copper kettle stood on a three-legged milking stool on the hearth.

The Summer days were now with us and it was a joy to walk around the airfield. Sometimes we disturbed a covey of partridges, with the mother bird leading her young. At our approach they would fly away with a flutter of wings. Meadowlarks hovered in the air singing joyously, the peewits made their funny cry and the crows cawed raucously. We loved our walks and I noticed, with the changing seasons, the variation of colour. First of all the primroses and violets appeared in the hedgerows and afterwards daisies and buttercups studded the grass. Sorrel, moon daises and wild thyme followed and so to Autumn, with its coloured foliage and blackberries, only to be replaced all too soon with a carpet of snow which stretched unbroken, glistening in the winter sunlight. Fan and I fed the birds on the balcony — we watched them greedily flutter down from their perches on the railings for the food, then fly away to eat it in safety on the airfield.

Periodically my father-in-law would come to stay. One of these visits was made during the winter months and the Control Tower was cold, as usual! Rob decided it was time to look for another form of heating (by this time we had bought a table model electric cooker which behaved better than the range). Eventually he bought a stove — a heavy black affair, box-like and solid — that would stay alight all night. Depositing it at the bottom of the stairs, Rob found that it was much too heavy to even contemplate carrying it upstairs. We stood and looked at the stove. I felt we were in much the same predicament as I was when the furniture arrived.

"There is one way," said Rob, "Get the rolling pin, put it under the stove and roll and lever the stove up the stairs."

This seemed so easy until we tried and found that the rolling pin was too short to balance the stove on.

The next attempt was made using a towel rail. Eventually, after a great many trials and tribulations, the stove finally reached the sitting room. Grandpa and Rob thoroughly enjoyed themselves dismantling the range. They worked hard and got very black. At last the stove was in place and the poor old range, which I'm sure had done its best, was banished to the basement.

Soon they had a fire going. The men then washed the grime from themselves and settled down to enjoy the warmth. I got Fan ready for bed, thinking longingly of sitting down in front of a good fire again and really getting warm. The Control Tower was at last beginning to heat up, if the roasted faces and self-satisfied expressions of the men were anything to go by. Gratefully I pushed my way towards the fire and sat down as close as I could to it. It really was hot! Down below the doorbell rang, followed by frantic hammering on the door.

Rob grumbled, "Just as we have got settled, someone is sure to come." He didn't hurry himself to go and answer. But the caller was now standing with a finger pressed firmly on the bell. Leisurely Rob left his wonderful fireside and equally as leisurely went downstairs. Minutes later he rushed past us and threw a bowl of water on the fire! We gazed through a cloud of smoke and ashes at him in astonishment. We were covered with fine white dust from the fire.

"What did you do that for?" I demanded furiously, "You must be mad, you've only just got it going!"

"We have to put it out," panted Rob, "We've got the chimney on fire! The sparks are blowing towards the farmer's straw ricks."

So much for trying to keep warm, I thought bitterly as we cleaned up the wet mess of ashes. We did eventually get everything under control and the Control Tower became warmer and more comfortable. My father-in-law's visit came to an end, and we were left alone again.

CHAPTER
SIXTEEN

It seemed very quiet with Rob at the office all day and only Fan for company, for I had no means of getting anywhere except by walking. Eventually our first occasion of formal entertaining arrived. It was someone we felt was quite important, and I wanted to create a good impression, but did not feel too confident! While Rob was out, I gave the furniture an extra polish, and gathered flowers from our garden, arranging them with care. At last everything was sparkling and nice, the best china, table-linen and cutlery were in readiness, and I began to plan the menu. It was a fairly simple meal. Nothing too ambitious, it was safer that way I thought. Roast meat and vegetables, followed by plum tart, cheese and biscuits and coffee. Nothing could go wrong — or could it?

Every year I had bottled fruit, made jams and pickles and altogether kept a good store cupboard, so I opened a jar of the best plums. The pastry for the pie was painstakingly rolled out, I did a few leaf decorations on top and the pie was popped into the electric oven in the kitchen. The meat and vegetables were done to a turn, the table looked inviting — we were all set for a successful visit!

We welcomed our guest and I left the men together while I proceeded to serve the first course. Although I say it myself, everything was cooked to perfection. The gravy was smooth (for once), not a lump to be seen. I settled back in my chair with a sigh of relief — everything was going to plan. There's nothing to this entertaining lark after all, I thought.

The time came to bring in the plum pie — it really did look appetising. I set it reverently on the table.

"Would our guest try a small portion?"

He would, if it was as delicious as the first course he was in for a treat, he said appreciatively. How true were his words! Smiling modestly I cut the first slice, plunged the spoon into the plums and out came, I gazed in horror, forgot my hostess manners and said in a loud voice, "Look — the ring from the plum jar!" There balanced precariously for all to see, even if I had not told them, was a large red rubber ring!

It just goes to show that when you try too hard to do everything perfectly, something will go wrong.

Life had had its moments at the Control Tower but Fan was now three years old and we felt it was time to move. The years spent there had been happy ones, full of experiences I would not have missed. So we began to look at houses and land for this time we were in a position to put a deposit on a house, or perhaps build a bungalow, with the aid of a mortgage.

While we were searching, the owner of the cottage my Aunt rented died and the house was now for sale. It seemed that this might be the answer to her problem and ours, for us to buy the cottage and move back there. The house needed quite a lot of modernisation and we knew we would have to do it ourselves, but it had possibilities and although it was not the home I had dreamed of, I felt glad that we would all be together.

We packed our belongings with mixed feelings. The Control Tower had been our first proper home and it held happy memories.

CHAPTER
SEVENTEEN

At the cottage, the work of the garden had been too much for my Aunt, even though she loved it and spent many happy hours there. Over many following years we shaped the garden. Rob cut down trees and cleared a space to plant vegetables — we also built a chicken run. Rob invested in some chickens (they were going to make our fortune), we fixed up a heater and hot water bottles to keep them warm, for they were expensive pure-bred day-old chicks. The small bundles of yellow fluff were falling over each other as they huddled in their boxes. They were newly hatched, so we chopped up hard-boiled eggs into minute pieces and dipped their beaks into the food and water to teach them how to eat and drink. Fan watched fascinated as they learned to feed and raised their downy heads as if saying grace.

They grew rapidly with the exception of one or two that were trampled by the more energetic ones. They thrived until one day I discovered blood and feathers in the chicken coop — overnight they had turned cannibal. 75% of them went that way, the remainder survived. We moved them into a larger run which Rob had built for them and they grew into fine birds. We were so proud of them, showing them to the guests that were staying with us at the time. I must say they saw them at their best for during the night the rain poured down in torrents, and in the morning I found, to my horror, that the poultry were half drowned. The roofing felt that covered the chicken coop had collected the rainwater and then burst, deluging them. The obvious thing was to move them to a dry place. If they were going to survive they had to be dried out quickly.

It was easy for me to stand there, in Rob's wellingtons, weighing up the situation. Putting it into practice was a very different thing! The wretched birds had to be caught and the only way to do it was to get in the coop with them. I crouched down and struggled into the coop — I was surrounded by wet and squawking fowls. Grabbing a handful of wet feathers I tucked a bird under my arm and gingerly began to shuffle forwards in a crouching position towards the door of the run. I was practically walking about inside the wellingtons, they flapped around my knees and I was weighed down with them as well as the hens!

Our guests were no doubt sitting peacefully by the window enjoying the pure fresh air of the countryside. It was the last they would get for some time, I thought fiendishly (that is if I ever got out of the coop with the stinking birds). I did not dare to think what would happen if a rat appeared! I am terrified of them. I finally got out of the coop and staggered down to the house with one wet hen. After a succession of many such trips I had managed to rescue all of the hens — I was nearly as exhausted as they were!

Everywhere indoors stank of wet feathers and hens — they were drying out in boxes all over the place and beginning to revive with the help of weak brandy and water which I forced into their beaks — it was not easy!

I am glad to say they recovered and a new run was made for them, this time in deep litter. They absolutely loved it and rewarded us with eggs — all was well until the day I returned to the hens, just after I had fed them, and found as many rats as hens tucking into the food! After that we disposed of the poultry — all our relatives got one "oven ready" for the pot. The rats were dealt with!

The deep litter house was converted into a greenhouse where we grew, untroubled by vermin, luscious tomatoes and cucumbers. We raised seedlings, and Fan, at a later date, kept a collection of cacti in it.

We were also working on the house. Rob had taken the copper and range out of the kitchen. A large dresser was converted into kitchen cupboards and working surfaces. Everything was painted a gay jasmine yellow and bright red. (The most diabolical colour scheme I could have chosen — visions of scrambled egg and tomato sauce!) An immersion heater and boiler were installed and in due course one of the larders was turned into a bathroom. Until this was done, we bathed in the kitchen, first of all staggering from the barn clutching a large galvanised tin bath. This was then filled with hot water from a series of kettles and saucepans and any other container we could muster. After our ablutions, we emptied the bath by bailing the water out and pouring it into the sink. Then we tilted the bath to catch the last drops, before sallying forth with the bath to hang it on its rusty nail in the barn until next time.

The day arrived when the bathroom was installed. It was all very cosy — the door opened directly into the sitting-room, so we could almost carry on a conversation or watch TV, but of course modesty prevailed!

Auntie's sitting-room was redecorated and a pair of French doors installed. The house was painted inside and out and gradually took on a bright appearance. The drab brown paint, so beloved by the Victorians, had been replaced with a cream colour. On the whole it was an enjoyable period, living back at the cottage. We had worked hard, but it wasn't my dream house — did one exist?

The years slipped by and our dream house was still only a figment of the imagination, "shelved" for the time being because we suddenly had the opportunity to become caravan owners!

CHAPTER
EIGHTEEN

Two caravans on the coast were for sale — we thought how lovely it would be to spend our holidays in them and sit back and count the lovely money rolling in from tenants, whom we felt sure couldn't wait to rent our vans.

One Easter weekend we set off to the Dorset coast to inspect the vans. The journey was lovely. I think I shall always remember my first impression of the New Forest — the gorse was in bloom and ponies grazed on the roadside, unafraid of the endless stream of traffic. The view stretched for miles, showing dense foliage interspersed with large expanses of heather. There were small water holes for the ponies and cattle to drink from and there were endless plants and places to explore another day when we had time to spare.

We came to the rolling Purbeck hills, in which nestled villages built with the local stone. We did not realise then what affection we would one day hold for that wonderful countryside. It opened up a whole new world to be enjoyed!

The sun glinted on Swanage Bay and everything was peaceful and dreaming. A few holiday-makers were coming into town and some no doubt would be staying in caravans. We found the caravan site and vans without any difficulties. One was an 18 foot 4 berth with an end kitchen, the other van was somewhat older and was 14 foot. They were sited in a lovely position overlooking the bay. It was a happy day for us when we bought them. Since that day we have had years of pleasure and hard work — but as Rob said, "You can't have one without the other!"

As each holiday season began we packed blankets and everything we needed and made our way to that now familiar coast. Sometimes the sun was shining; at other times, when Easter was early in the year, we shivered — it even snowed once. On that occasion we sat miserably in the van with our feet on hot water bottles, for caravans in those days were not the luxurious holiday homes they are now. If we were lucky and the sun shone, we painted the vans and spread the cushions on the grass to air and generally got the vans ready for the holiday season. In the Autumn we packed everything away for the winter and took all the bedding home with us to be washed, to return yet again in the Spring.

We saw the countryside in all its changing moods. At Eastertide the gorse was in bloom, and prolific primroses and violets nestled in the hedgerows and on grassy banks. Much later in the year vast hedges of rhododendrons bloomed and later still, the trees turned to bronze and gold. We enjoyed the beauty of all the seasons. Corfe Castle rose majestically between the great breast of hill that dominated the scene. Away across the fields to Windspit and Kimmeridge Bay, we came to the sea again and utter peace, which only the raucous cries of the sea gulls disturbed.

We made friends with other caravan owners and at the beginning of each season we would greet each other like long lost friends and catch up on all the winter news.

CHAPTER
NINETEEN

The search for our dream home was resumed. One November day Rob told me he had seen two derelict cottages in a village a few miles away, in Warwickshire. It was a grey November day when he took me to see them. They were built of local stone, the thatch was falling badly from the roofs and from a broken window a dirty curtain flapped. Weeds grew in profusion — even on the thatch — and quite frankly I could not see them transformed, even with a great stretch of my imagination, into the house of my dreams. Granted the position was ideal, for the cottages faced onto a broad sweep of village green, but that was all there was in their favour, or so I thought! My husband was more far-seeing than I. He could visualise all the possibilities that existed. "Let's go home," I said unkindly, "They are a waste of time." Rob looked disappointed and he began to wonder just what I did want.

We were still house-hunting in the Spring, and by this time I was having second thoughts about the cottages. "Let's go back to look at the cottages again," I suggested to Rob. This time the sun was shining as we walked across the village green. We pushed open the creaking gate and fought our way through the jungle of nettles, elder bushes and thistles to the rear of the cottages. Then a strange thing happened, everything fell into place for there was the garden, stretching, I could hardly believe it, towards an orchard. The fruit trees were in full bloom, and oh the sheer beauty of it all, the sun-cast shadows beneath the trees on the lush green grass and the pink and white blossom that had floated gently down to the ground.

We called on the owner and there we met with disappointment, for a deposit for the cottages had been accepted only that week. Sadly we returned home — the cottages however still beckoned and in desperation Rob wrote to the owner and asked for first refusal, if for any reason the sale went off.

Weeks passed and then it happened! A letter arrived from the owner. The prospective purchaser had withdrawn the offer, were we still interested? We certainly were! Eventually the preliminaries were over, we had paid a deposit and once again, as we had done when we went to the Control Tower, we drank to our future.

The usual time elapsed before the purchase was completed. We were then at last able to take our gardening tools with us and chop down the weeds in the overgrown garden. What treasures we found, roses and currant bushes long since reverted to nature, and beautiful old stones, which had been used to edge the flower borders years ago. Inside the cottages there was a wealth of old beams blackened with age and vast inglenook fireplaces could be seen. I looked through the dirty window panes across the village green to the duckpond and beyond to the mellow stone houses. I tried to visualise our new home and hoped that it would fit in with the surroundings.

As the weeks passed, so we planted bulbs and new fruit trees in the orchard. In a little dell at the edge of the orchard we planted primroses and blue and white field violets. We enjoyed many happy, if somewhat strenuous, hours as we cut down the undergrowth. We sampled the soft fruits which, despite being almost choked with weeds, still managed to produce gooseberries and currants. We cooked becon and egg on a primus stove in the open air, and later, tired after so much work in the fresh air, made our way home where Rob would get on with drawing the plans for the house. We discussed colour schemes and garden lay-out — in fact we lived, ate and breathed, we even dreamed of our new project!

At last the plans were completed and passed. Builders began to dismantle the two cottages, for alas they were too dangerous to be preserved, but before the rebuilding could take place, it was Winter again and we had months of snow and ice; for it turned out to be the longest and most severe winter we had for a number of years.

Months passed, but finally the great day came when we were able to see the foundations laid and the walls slowly rise. Rooms began to take shape; how small they appeared to be, but we measured and found the builders had been accurate. Someday, however deceptively small they appeared to be now, they would be spacious and comfortable. Each evening became an adventure, to explore and see all that had been achieved during the day. We picked our way among the rubble and through the doorframe openings to stare through non-existent glass across the village green.

In the Spring — climbing over yet more builders' rubble in our future garden — we picked daffodils which we had planted the previous Autumn. Our new fruit trees bloomed and the Spring days passed all too fast, giving way to Summer. The apples had set on the fruit trees in the orchard and we hoped that by the time the fruit gathering season came around we would be installed in "Little Orchard". In the hall Fan carved her name and the date on one of the bricks before the plaster was put on walls — I thought that perhaps in years to come someone would find that brick and wonder whose name was carved there and why. Other people would live out their lives there and the trees and shrubs we had planted would one day bear their fruits and flowers for others. How true my thoughts were — if only I had known!

On one of our many visits we were pleased to see that the scaffolding had been erected and work on the upstairs walls had begun. Rob climbed the ladder, which had conveniently been left by the builders.

"Come on up," Rob invited, "There is a lovely view from the windows."

Placing my foot tentatively on the bottom rung of the ladder, and with my heart full of misgivings, I slowly climbed.

"You'll be all right." said my ever-loving encouragingly, "Give me your hand."

Trustingly I let go of the ladder and, with a heave from Rob, I was standing by his side.

"Now," he instructed, "Be careful not to stand on the edge of the boards, or you will go down quicker than you came up!"

With that comforting thought I slowly edged my way along the scaffolding boards. Rob was right, the view from the window was lovely — I looked across the village nestling in the midst of its green hills. In fact I got quite carried away with the thought of living in such a beautiful place — and that's when I forgot and looked down! What a mistake!

"I can't stay up here another minute!" I said.

"Why not?" said Rob unfeelingly, "You may as well see the rest of it now you are up here. This will be the bathroom." he said with the air of a tourist guide.

"I don't care what it will be — I know I shall never get down — just look at the drop into the hall!" I said.

Then it began to rain heavily and my best coat had been left in what one day would be the kitchen. I was getting wet. This was when I decided to remain calm. Mind you, there was not much alternative, so I placed my foot on the far-side rung of the ladder and then the great moment came to take my other foot off the non-existent landing! Well, I made it and what a relief it was to be on the ground floor again.

The house progressed rapidly — indeed interested spectators said they had never seen anything like it. The bricks and stones literally flew into place. In view of this all the timber was ordered. That's when everything started to go wrong.

80

The timber reclined on the village green joined by sand and cement and all the other equipment the builders needed. Unfortunately, this coincided with the village fête, which was traditionally held on the village green. We were given due warning that it would really upset the "bowling for the pig" if our materials were not moved as this, it seemed, was the one level spot. Rob promised to have a word with the builder. The builder agreeably promised to move the timber and we hoped a tidy-up would take place before the day of the fête. Some of the timber was moved and stacked behind the house and all but a corner of the green, where the wheel of fortune was supposed to stand, was tidied. However, our popularity, if we had any to start with, declined still further when a load of sand was delivered and tipped on the corner of the green, just before the fête.

The fête was duly held, even if the "bowling for the pig" took place higher up on the green than before. Tactfully we kept away, only returning to view our new home when all the festivities were over and the remains of the fête cleared away.

Work progressed slowly and all hope of being installed in our new home during the Summer months were dashed. Even our plans for entertaining visitors at "Little Orchard" in the Autumn were due to be disappointed. Actually, there was nothing to stop us having guests to stay at the cottage, but we only had three bedrooms and they were all in use. Rob and I found it rather trying to sleep for any length of time on the sitting-room floor, even though we had airbeds to lie on. It was also a bit much having to make sure we were up, dressed and our beds cleared away before the visitors came downstairs for breakfast. As much as we loved having people to stay, we were always glad to see them leave so we could get a good night's sleep!

One of our guests was most thoughtful — we had as usual settled down for an uncomfortable night on our air beds when the sitting-room door stealthily opened and by the flickering fire light we saw a cap and boots appear.

"Sorry to trouble you," said the voice apologetically, "I've just got to go out to the back." (This being our primitive earth closet — a two-seater situated, in good old country style, at the top of the first garden.) Attired for the keen night air, at least he had not had to dress in a hurry it seemed, he carefully climbed over our reclining forms, unlocked the back door and disappeared, with speed, into the darkness! Minutes dragged by, all thought of settling down to sleep was postponed. Rob began to look worried.

"Do you think he is all right?" he asked.

"Well, *I* can hardly go and see!" I retorted sarcastically.

"I'll give him a little longer." said Rob generously. Or could it have been that he did not want to wander up the garden on a cold dark night, I wondered. Eventually Rob draped himself in a dressing gown, donned slippers and sallied forth to investigate, only to return looking thoughtful.

"He's not there." he said Visions of what could happen with a two-seater, on a cold dark night, were clearly going through his mind. Rob shuffled upstairs and there, tucked up in our bed, sleeping peacefully, the sleep of one who had done his duty well, was the missing guest.

The morning revealed that while our guest had been "meditating", it had suddenly struck him that it would be more thoughtful if he returned via my Aunt's sitting-room, so that we would not be disturbed a second time. "In fact," he said airily, "It was a great pity I had not thought of it in the first place." Weakly we agreed!

CHAPTER
TWENTY

Complications with the building set in with a vengeance — work at "Little Orchard" was delayed, workmen changed, others took over. We watched the roof felt and battens go into place — then there were delivery delays. We began to plan to do the work ourselves.

One Saturday morning Rob set off to meet the builder and to "lend a hand", to speed thing up. He planned to lay some of the floorboards on the first floor. I was surprised to see him back home at 1 o'clock. Rob explained he was on his way to buy some nails, the builder had failed to arrive and there were just two men there fixing the porch. Rob was not happy!

That afternoon Fan and I armed with hammers and a bag of nails joined Rob at "Little Orchard". Carefully he and Fan climbed the ladder, walked along the rafters and began to lay the floorboards. By the end of the day a third of the floor had been laid, with the help of two car jacks (Rob did not possess floor cramps). Wearily we piled into the car and made our way back to the cottage. I had not done much to help — my job was to pass up boards as needed — so when Sunday arrived and the "workers" were eager to return to their labours,

I decided the time had come for me to be up there with them!

We stuffed two ancient hot water bottles with old nylons, as Fan and Rob had found it rather hard on their knees, kneeling for so long on bare boards. It was with great trepidation that I again climbed the ladder. It was a bit of an effort getting down into a comfortable position with my hammer and nails, but at least I was able to hammer away happily. Until Fan, who was below, reported that the nails I had knocked in were not in the joists at all. I went back to my day-dreaming.

There were times, though, when my dreaming took a practical turn — having planned colour schemes for each room, all I had to do was find the right materials and floor-coverings. This was optimistic to say the least as we were on a very tight budget. However, one day, when I was poring over yet another magazine on house furnishing, I read of some hard-wearing felt that could be obtained straight from the mills, at a fraction of the cost we had expected to pay for carpet. It was luck indeed, for the mill was not far from home. One fine morning Rob, Fan and I set off to visit the little market town where the mill was situated. There were only about three factories there. We came to North Mill and were taken upstairs to see the felt, vast rolls of brown, fawn, cinnamon or white. The possibilities for the white were endless. It could be dyed and used for curtains, upholstery, floor-covering and all sorts of things. The white felt had to be ordered, it was so popular, and no more would be coming off the rollers till Friday week. We had originally planned to go to the caravans at

Swanage that weekend, but we felt justified in losing a day of our holiday in the circumstances.

We were able to take enough brown felt home with us to cover the stairs, landing and the sitting room. We ordered sufficient white felt to cover the bedroom floors and make curtains for the sitting room. It was a good bargain being the by-product of another commodity and therefore sold at a reasonable price. Now it was possible for us to have wall-to-wall floor-covering — this exceeded our wildest dreams!

I then started to search for curtain materials for all the windows, with the exception of the sitting room, where I hoped the white felt — suitably dyed — would be used. Again luck was with me — a market stall was selling reject cotton and brocade at a fraction of the normal cost. The pieces were at least six foot in length and equally as wide, which was ideal for large windows. I bought enough for all the curtains and extra to make bedspreads, drape dressing tables and cover bedroom stools. I was able to co-ordinate room colours and felt well pleased with the results. Although there were flaws in the materials, they were difficult to see, so I was very satisfied with my efforts.

Then all three of us went down with flu — in rotation — and everything connected with "Little Orchard" was postponed. It was three weeks before we were well enough to visit it again. We were thrilled to see everything that had been done, as we picked our way through the remains of the concrete the builders had left.

The sunlight filtered through the newly glazed windows, the wood door in the hall had been hung and the electricians had done the first part of the wiring for the plugs and lights. The plugs were partly fixed. Aunt produced a tape measure and began to measure her rooms for the furniture she intended to bring with her. We had built a kitchen, sitting room and bedroom for her use, so that she would feel she had her own little house. We climbed the ladder again, for as yet we had no stairs. My Aunt, not to be outdone (at 82 years of age), also climbed so that she could see her bedroom!

As the weeks passed the house began to get to a really interesting stage. The plastering was finally finished, but not before Rob, with the help of Fan, had fixed a lovely beam in readiness for Aunt's fireplace. He also found the original blue flagstones from the floor of the old cottages, which he used to make a hearth. It was amazing to see just how wide the chimney breast appeared, the walls were satin smooth and we were satisfied and pleased with the result.

The kitchen sink had arrived, but not the rest of the kitchen units. The sink was a blue glazed ceramic one and we planned to have grey unit tops and grey striped curtains.

CHAPTER
TWENTY-ONE

Christmas came and went and the January snows were with us — it was bitterly cold so we were unable to work at "Little Orchard" at the weekends. Later the bulbs bravely began to poke their way through the soil in the orchard, giving the promise that Spring was not far away. Optimistically we felt that we should be installed this year before Summer came round again. We began painting the window frames, but the weather was so cold we were clutching the brushes with icy fingers — Rob, who had gone outside onto the scaffolding, soon came indoors again. February was bright and sunny allowing us to get quite a lot of work done, and not only during the day for now we had electricity and could work in the evenings. We took an electric fire with us and so we were warm as well.

During the day the orchard had a resident — in the form of a grey squirrel. Whether he was one of a family or a lone squirrel, we did not know, but he sat on his haunches in solitary splendour, with his lovely bushy tail arching gracefully. He watched us and seemed to "sum us up" — I don't think he liked us, as he bounded away across the branches very speedily and was soon lost from sight among the fruit trees.

Our lives seemed to be completely dominated by houses in one form or another, in Rob's work he dealt with them all day long, then there was the cottage and "Little Orchard", not forgetting the caravans. We disposed of the smaller van which cut down the work, and although one dream seemed to be coming true, or so we thought, there were moments when Rob and I looked forward to the day when all the work was completed and we should have a little time to visit friends again. It seemed so long since we had relaxed. Occasionally we had visitors to chat to us while we worked, but as one said, as he departed, "If you have five minutes to spare, don't spend it with someone who hasn't!"

We were still some way off completing all the work that had to be done at "Little Orchard", but the bathroom fittings had been ordered, and we thought things were taking shape at last. Rob had arranged to be at the house when the bathroom fittings arrived, to take delivery, but unfortunately he was too late. The first thing that met his astonished gaze was one pale blue bath, two WC pedestals (one blue and one white) and a blue wash basin — all reclining on the village green. Also 14 bags of glass fibre, which nestled costly next to all the bathroom fittings. There wasn't a workman in sight! Rob hastily opened the front door and embracing the WC pedestals one at a time, he struggled indoors with them. He then manoeuvred the washbasin inside and the 14 bags of fibreglass. The bath was too much for him single-handed so he covered it discreetly with a tarpaulin, hoping it would blend in with the countryside until the evening, when he optimistically thought we could both go over and move it indoors between us

Armed with the rolling pin — the largest we possessed — we arrived at the house and prepared to do battle! The bath was still shrouded with the tarpaulin, and looked rather sinister as it reposed in the dim light on the village green. We unlocked the front door, where we found another surprise — all the kitchen units had arrived! They had obviously been delivered since Rob's visit and someone had thoughtfully forced open the temporary back door and deposited them any old where! Eventually we made room for the bath, then we placed the rolling pin under its tilted end and we rolled and pushed and pulled the bath slowly towards the front door. At last it was safely in the hall and we were more than relieved. Pausing to get our breath back, we admired the new fittings, although we were hardly in a fit state to admire anything. We managed to summon up enough energy to hurl the 14 bags of fibreglass onto the landing, in readiness for the plumber.

Much later that evening Rob went out to the car to collect something. On his way back he noticed a further pile on the Green — this too had been covered over. It was the staircase! We had carried as much as we could indoors, but the staircase was impossible, it would have to wait until the following day, when we hoped the builders would deal with it. At last we came to the end of a tiring, but eventful day and wearily went back to the cottage and bed.

The following Monday Rob decided to look in at "Little Orchard" to see that all was well, for we had not been that weekend — someone having messed the lock up! All was well — there stacked in the front porch, overlapping the public footpath, were 85 sheets of plasterboard, a white glazed sink (complete with brackets) and also some copper tubing. To complete the picture, someone had industriously covered it with the ever-useful tarpaulin! Rob could not believe it — he was sure he had not ordered any plasterboard. What was more to the point we didn't need any! The sink, brackets and copper tube were ours but that was all. The lock was still jammed and there was a little note, which had been pushed half way underneath the front door, which read "Back in 20 minutes"!

Evidently someone intended to do something at sometime. It was all very frustrating. Rob had to continue on his way. He returned later to get yet another shock! Everything had disappeared, no trace of it remained. At this point my husband began to wonder if he was working too hard. But all was later revealed. The builder had returned, repaired the lock and had moved everything indoors, including the plasterboard, which he had neatly stacked with all the building materials that were ours!

One glorious Spring day we packed tea and Rob, Fan and I set off to work in the garden of "Little Orchard". We had not been able to devote much time to it recently, but now we explored all the corners and discovered a nice old stone path and a patch of bluebells. We could imagine its former design and we planned where our own plants and shrubs would be planted. Sitting on the backdoor step in the sunshine, we ate our tea, pausing from our labours to dream awhile.

The neighbour's garden was bright with daffodils and very shortly ours would be bright with weeds if it was left to its own devices. The orchard seemed full of life and movement — not only were there birds singing, but the squirrel had returned, this time bringing a companion with him. He darted from tree to tree, then, when he reached a branch that afforded him splendid isolation he would eat greedily. Our presence did not frighten him, nor did the two guinea fowl, who were perched in a nearby tree, deter him. Having finished his refreshments, he proceeded to have a fine old game of leaping from branch to branch — this showed off his bushy tail to perfection! His companion, quite unimpressed, played in the long grass beneath the trees.

On the village pond small boys were sailing their toy boats and weekend spectators stopped their cars to admire the quiet beauty and serenity of the village. It was surprising how often the empty house attracted passers-by — for the large windows gave a wonderful view inside and we received several enquiries to see if it was for sale. Cars stopped outside and the occupants watched with interest as we crouched on windowsills painting or struggled up and down ladders. It did have its lighter moments too — one evening when Rob was closing the windows at the front of the house he spotted a little man hands clasped in front of his best navy blue suiting. He gazed at the house for a few minutes, then he disappeared from view. He hadn't gone far, because when Rob went into the next room to shut the window in there, a face appeared at the window and a voice said. "Nice bit of stonework you've done, but modern, ent it?" Regretfully the little man shook his head and went on his way. I could see his point, for we would have liked to preserve the original cottages had they have been in a safe condition.

CHAPTER
TWENTY-TWO

I thought it would be a good idea to dye the felt in readiness for covering the floors, so with my shopping list I sallied forth. Buying the cold water dye was simple. Back at the cottage we cleaned a large galvanised dustbin. Placing the bin on a platform of bricks in the garden, we filled it with water and added the carpet dye. Then we lit a fire under the dustbin to heat the mixture. Hauling the felt into the bin we attempted to turn it and open it out, so it would colour evenly. We were in trouble! The felt fitted snugly into the bin and it was hopeless to try and move it around. There was only one thing to do, tip out the water and felt, refill the dustbin and start all over again. It was beginning to get expensive. This time, with the fresh dye, we took the corners of the felt, and soaked it a piece at a time. It began to take the dye and a lovely blue was the result.

We then met trouble — too much felt and not enough dye, so the results were patchy. We staggered to the clothes-line with the sodden felt and began to drape it over the line. The line snapped and we had to pick up all the wet material from the ground before it spoiled. It was not a success, but we didn't give up — we decided to cut smaller pieces and dye them separately, but first we took the offending felt we had dyed to "Little Orchard", spreading it on one of the bedroom floors to complete the drying process. The room smelt terrible for days, though the felt finally dried out leaving the floorboards a kind of blue colour!

More dye was bought, for we did not have nearly enough, and Rob built the brick platform higher and this time put the primus stove in the middle, instead of a fire, placing the dustbin on top. We mixed the dye and stirred the felt round and round. Now the first small piece was dyed, so we struggled into the bathroom with it (what a blessing the bathroom was downstairs). This time we were going to do the job properly, so we rinsed and rinsed the dyed fabric in plenty of cold water — we felt quite pleased: success at last, for we now had a rich royal blue felt, which this time we were able to peg on the line to dry. In fact we were doing so well we became quite carried away with our success. We dyed four more pieces of carpet, then four more pieces for heavy curtains. The last item to be dyed was a bedspread, which turned out a lovely powder blue, because by now the dye was losing its strength. Every available line was filled and as the evening was almost over we groped our way in the dusk to put up yet another clothes-line. Soon the felt was blowing gently in the breeze. We hoped the weather would remain fine and I hastily turned my thoughts away from the possibility of rain — for one awful moment, the picture of the felt once again in the mud seemed to float before my eyes.

At 1.00am we had thankfully locked the door for the night, our labours at and end, or so we thought! For upon opening the bathroom door we found water seeping from under the bath, blue water to be exact, and the bath still half full, the drain being well and truly blocked. Rob wearily unlocked the back door to the garden and began to free the waste pipe. I mopped up water, but since we were both so tired and it was far too dark to do much, we left it until the morning — slightly blue in more ways than one we made our way supperless to bed!

In the morning half the felt was dry. Though some pieces were patchy, the bedspread was a success.

After all our labours we felt we badly needed a holiday, so once again we packed the caravan equipment and departed for Swanage.

It was lovely to see the now all-too-familiar countryside in all its beauty. The gorse was in full bloom and here and there were patches of yellow broom. Clumps of wild campion and blue bells were in the hedgerows and woodlands. There was wild parsley and the fields were golden with buttercups. It was a beautiful time of year.

Swanage was peaceful and all was restful until the seagulls decided to parade on the caravan roof early the next morning. We decided to rise early, cook breakfast, pack a picnic and go to Kimmeridge Bay. There we lay in the sunshine and felt, at last, that we were really on holiday.

Our break ended all to soon, but refreshed we returned to the cottage and confusion. Boxes we had packed ready for removal were piled on top of each other. The garden was bare of plants, for the roses had been lifted and moved to "Little Orchard". Our dear old Bramley apple tree, which over the years had borne prolifically, was once again promising a bumper crop of fruit. I felt sad, for memories of my life at the cottage stretched back further than Rob's, and I wondered what life would hold in store for us at "Little Orchard" would the years deal kindly, as they had done at the cottage — I wondered?

In the week we had been away the nettles had grown again in our new garden, but the garden would have to wait. The day before we moved, Rob laid the felt floor covering at "Little Orchard". The sitting room came up to expectations for we used the thick brown felt. The blue and white felt for the bedrooms was disappointing. The blue felt now showed four distinct shades, which made us realise that all our efforts had been in vain — we had no alternative but to lay our old carpets on top of the felt, so only a felt surround showed.

The day came when a large van arrived at "Little Orchard", and all the furniture, with the exception of a large Victorian wardrobe, was soon in place. The wardrobe would not go up the staircase, but with the help of a ladder and ropes it was slowly hoisted through the bedroom window. When the removal men had gone, we worked long and hard and at midnight we at last climbed into bed. We had not had time to hang the curtains, which would have deadened the noise of the traffic that changed gear on its way up the steep hill some distance behind our house. Everything seemed strange, but as Rob remarked, somewhat misguidedly I thought, "It's just like a holiday, isn't it?" I must admit I was not entirely "with him", but then I had never felt so exhausted in my life and I had never spent a holiday moving furniture!

By the next weekend most of the furniture had been arranged to our satisfaction. Poor Rob and Fan had moved the bedroom suite into another room and brought the furniture from the guest room into our bedroom, where it seemed to fit so much better. Gradually the house began to take on the look of "home", although it did not seem quite like the cottage — but at least it was easier work-wise. We still had a few empty spaces to fill and as there was an auction sale a few miles away, we planned to arrive in good time to view all the furniture we had marked in the catalogue.

There were the usual group of bargain hunters waiting for the sale to begin. As we joined them I gazed longingly at a gate-legged table and three-piece suite we hoped we would be lucky enough to buy. At last they came under the hammer, and they were ours! I had spent a sleepless night the day before the sale, planning what we should buy, and I spent another sleepless night after the sale, planning where we should place the furniture. At last I realised it was no good. Furniture and colour schemes were flitting through my mind in a never-ending fashion. I decided I had better let my mind go blank — a thing I had no difficulty doing in an emergency! It was only at night that my brain seemed to be galvanised into action! I was furious with myself and fed up. Why couldn't I get some sleep? It was at this point Rob gave a groan and staggered out of bed.

Flouncing over and turning on the light, I enquired peevishly, "What's the matter now?" Rob was crouched on the side of the bed, in a very funny position indeed. His face was contorted with pain and mine was distorted with frustration! (Never mind the nights I kept the poor uncomplaining soul awake with my tossing and turning.) Rob was busily rubbing his leg as if his life depended on it.

"Cramp!" he gasped.

"Oh, is that all!" I said, unsympathetically as I switched off the light, leaving him to his suffering, in darkness. I was going to get some sleep if it killed me. For the next half hour all I could hear was a steady "rub-rub" (just like sand paper on the wood we were preparing for painting — as if we had not had enough of that!), oohs and aahs, followed by more rubbing, until finally he tumbled into bed exhausted. Towards morning we both drifted into an uneasy slumber. The next day the furniture arrived from the saleroom and it was all that we could have wished for!

The garden still yielded nettles and there were large lumps of soil where the ground had been disturbed for the main drainage to be put in. I was thrilled to see that two of the shrubs that we had moved from the cottage, and which to all appearances had been just dead twigs, now had beautiful new shoots forming. A promise of things to come. The young trees also showed promise: one of them had three rosy apples, another had seven apples, but on the third tree the blossom had not set.

Again we planted more bulbs in the orchard and I was able to buy some magnificent Autumn Crocus, as they are commonly known, which we planted while they were in full bloom. They continued to flower and gave pleasure as an abundance of flowers unfolded beneath the trees.

The weather was dry and warm, the flowers we had left at the cottage now looked decidedly worse for wear, so hastily we cleared a patch of ground at "Little Orchard", then we could transplant them and give them the water and attention they required. It was a miracle the poor things had survived at all, their roots were dry as we lifted them from the soil, so dry it fell in powder to the ground. Rob and I filled the boot of the car with plants. We tied the large, half-grown purple lilacs to the roof rack, and returned to "Little Orchard". The holes we had dug in readiness for the plants we partly filled with water, then spreading the roots evenly, we firmed the soil around the plants and gave them a long drink of water. After a week or so they had taken on a new lease of life — although one or two still looked poorly. Experience had taught us it was best to plant three of each species if possible, and that plants that were not fully grown would establish themselves more easily.

At the foot of the wall of our new house, near the porch, we planted a fine red rose, which at a later date climbed over the stonework and bloomed in profusion. In the corner of the front garden we placed a flowering cherry tree, which had been a Mothering Sunday gift from Fan. We surrounded the narrow strip of front garden with a low stone wall, leaving crevices for aubrietia and various rock plants, which we hoped would supply a cascade of colour. At the base of the walls Rob had built we planted mimulus and gentians.

At the back of the house, in the orchard, the squirrels had been helping themselves to the Filbert nuts — the shells lay under the trees. One of the squirrels, a fine big fellow, was sitting on the garden seat which we had placed under the ancient apple trees. He was enjoying his breakfast of nuts — I wished so much that I could have photographed him.

Rob was now building a fuel store. He had laid the foundations, using the stone that was left over from the old cottages, which was still lying around. We seemed to walk around with downcast eyes as we searched for suitable building stone. When we found one we added it to the pile, which lay in readiness for Rob to sort and fit into place. After only a short time, an elegant stone wall began to take shape — the first wall of the fuel shed! It was then, so full of enthusiasm, that we ran out of sand. We ordered some more, only to find that it had arrived when we were out and had been tipped in the driveway. It blocked the entrance to the rear of the house, and also took up the parking space for the car. Entrance by the other side of the house was well and truly blocked with left-over tiles — we had no rear or side access at all.

Visitors arrived for the afternoon, just one of those social gatherings — afternoon tea and all that! We also had another visitor — a little man who asked if we had any scrap metal to dispose of SCRAP METAL — there was an unsightly heap of old iron bedsteads, bicycles and what have you that we had dug up reclining at the other end of the garden. The little man looked as if he had struck gold, as we described in glowing terms the items we wanted to get rid of. He placed his foot on the heap of sand, as if he was about to climb Mount Everest, then he practically lost sight of his feet. With difficulty he extricated himself, and shaking the sand from his trouser legs, he departed, promising to call again the following Monday when, we assured him, the sand would have been moved. Needless to say that was the last we saw of him! We shovelled sand, rushing indoors at intervals to our other visitors, assuring them, with false promises, that we would not be too long.

The following weekend, as if we had not had enough of sand, we decided to make a hasty trip to Swanage to close the caravan for the season. It had been a Summer where we had seen very little of the sea, for there had been so much to do. All the old magic of Swanage was there, peaceful now that the Summer visitors had gone — the deserted beach, the gentle sound of the sea and far-off lights in the distance. We said good-bye for yet another year, with thoughts that may be next year there would be more time to be in dear Dorset.

CHAPTER
TWENTY-THREE

As the evenings grew darker, our thoughts turned again to the many indoor tasks that awaited us. Rob reminded me that the floorboards on the landing needed a few more nails. This he generously said was a job he could do on his own. Fan and I were only too pleased to leave him happily hammering nails in and we eagerly seized the opportunity to watch television for a change. It was so lovely to relax. We turned the electric fire on, determined to make ourselves comfortable and wallow in the unaccustomed leisure. For a full five minutes we gloated on our good fortune. Suddenly we were plunged into darkness — the electric fire and television picture faded — Rob had hit an electric wire that ran beneath the floorboards!

Groping our way to the door in the direction of the stairs, finally with the aid of a torch, we espied Rob. We crouched with our little light while he prised up the floorboards, which only a few minutes ago he had nailed down thoroughly (no half measures for him!). Finally we found the right floorboard and there, clearly to be seen, was a nail right through the electric wire. It was at least an hour before we were organised again.

As the 5th of November approached, the children who lived in the village built a huge bonfire on the village green. All the surplus rubbish was carried out — old broken down furniture and cast-off clothing collected by a house-to-house collection — and was stacked with great care. What fun the children had as they paraded in Mr. Someone-or-Other's jacket or Mrs. What-you-call-it's discarded Sunday hat! Later, when their interest had waned, they added it all to the bonfire, which was fast becoming very large indeed.

At long last 7.00pm came and promptly, with great ceremony, the fire was lit. Children and parents assembled at a safe distance to watch the flames as they leaped high in the air, almost reaching the splendid guy, who was balanced precariously right on the top of the pile. We had a ringside seat indoors. We switched off the lights and drew back the curtains so we could watch the fun.

It was lovely to see all the children clutching "sparklers", running hither and thither while anxious parents kept a watchful eye on them. As the fireworks were ignited, the flames leapt higher, and the silhouette of the crowd stood out sharply against the night sky. Fan was there. She had taken a potato to cook in the bonfire — a potato she was unable to find again amidst all the excitement. All too soon, however, the 5th of November was over for another year and suddenly Winter was upon us. All thoughts of gardening ceased. The ground was hard and it glistened with frost. Cobwebs clung in intricate patterns and lacy strands to the rose bushes and shrubs. Trees stood stark and black, outlined against the grey Winter sky. The grass was a white carpet and weak sunshine filtered through the bare branches to present a scene which is often seen on Christmas cards. Once again, I stood and admired the beauty of stone houses, their roofs now white.

This year we planned to spend Christmas in our new home. We decorated the rooms with holly and evergreens. It was a happy and peaceful time. On Boxing Day, quietly and stealthily the snow fell — children romped on the village green, now white, throwing snowballs, building snowmen and generally enjoying themselves, their cheeks glowing rosily from the cold and exercise. In the orchard, the prints of a fox could be seen clearly. He had come along the garden path and around the house, no doubt searching for food.

At last Spring arrived, weeds began to sprout in the garden and the nettles took over again! Would they never die? It seemed that the nettle roots stretched for miles and convulvulus flourished tenaciously, but somehow, amidst all the weeds, our plants lived and bloomed. We planted yet more rock plants. The mimulus and gentians we interspersed with dianthus and rock phlox. The results were all that we had imagined!

Now the fuel store was completed, Rob began to build the garage — he was using the stone from the old lavatories which, as is the custom, were situated right at the bottom of the garden. Everything within reason was utilised — he cleared bricks, which served the double purpose of clearing the ground of the debris as well as providing building materials. As he dismantled the two-seater building, he found that a starling had taken up residence and was rearing her young, so for a time work ceased until the birds had flown.

The months sped by. It did not feel as if we had been in the village for almost a year, and that it would soon be time for the village fête to be held again. This year the bowling for the pig would take place in its accustomed position on the green as it was now no longer littered with our building materials. I was delighted to be asked to help with the homemade cake stall. We did a brisk trade and very soon we had sold out! The sun shone and everyone enjoyed themselves. The children gave a display of country dancing — it was a typical village scene, that renews itself time and again.

I thought how beautiful the village looked, with its fine old Church sitting at the top of the hill — there were a great many steps to climb if the "short way" to it was preferred. The village lay out below as one paused for breath and looked down on the mellowed stone houses, nestling in the valley. You could see the green, with its duck pond glistening in the sunlight, water-lilies pink, yellow and white floating on the pond, ducks waddling across the road to dive with an ungainly plop to swim amongst the water lilies, searching for small insect life. It was a scene to remember!

Often I would open the door at "Little Orchard" to find a posy lying on the step, sometimes there would be fruit and vegetables too, but the nicest gift of all, one which I treasure the memory of, was a spray of strawberry leaves, which had turned to a most beautiful shade of pinkish red. I was told afterwards that they had been taken indoors and washed free from soil, as it rained the previous night. The leaves surrounded some of the old pink monthly roses and the colour blended so marvellously. Not just the beauty of the flowers touched my heart, but the thought and care which had gone into the gift. They had come from a real old country garden of old-fashioned flowers that was tended by two dear people who were a wealth of information of days gone by. I am sure their passing left a gap in the village, never to be filled.

I shall always remember the wise words of one of them: It was at the time Rob had become ill and had been rushed with acute pain to hospital. It was a pain we did not know the cause of and my days passed as if in a dream. All my feelings seemed numb, but the wise words "This too will pass" proved both a comfort and right. It's still something I hold onto in times of stress. So the worries passed — Rob was soon home again, better but not quite his usual self.

CHAPTER
TWENTY-FOUR

Rob was recovering from his illness, but unfortunately our strength seemed to be running out. I wasn't too well, the years had gone and by now we had to face the fact that we were not getting any younger. Everything took on enormous proportions so eventually we decided the sensible thing to do was to move into a bungalow — something easy, with a more manageable garden and preferably nearer Fan, who was now happily married and lived in a village a few miles away.

Reluctantly we decided to put "Little Orchard" on the market. We had realised our dreams and built our house, an experience we would not have missed. The house was duly advertised and after some months it was finally sold. Strangely enough, our feelings were of relief — it had been a great achievement to build our own house, seeing it take shape, a permanent landmark of our own design — but now it was time to move on.

We moved to an easily run bungalow in a village near to Fan. Again the garden was in a wild state, for at some time or other it had been part of an orchard. Now the orchard was a small estate of houses and bungalows. The front of ours was open-plan, but the rear garden had been fenced — there wasn't a stone wall in sight!

The accommodation consisted of three bedrooms, bathroom (with separate WC), a kitchen that was all of ten foot square and had a door leading straight into the garage and fuel store, a sitting room of a reasonable size. However, we incorporated the third bedroom and had French windows installed in it. Central heating was also put in — that was the extent of the alterations indoors.

The garden was a different matter. We had to begin again! We dug flower beds and borders all on solid clay. We then sallied forth to an auction sale of trees and shrubs — the result was even more rewarding than I had anticipated, even with my love of trees and shrubs. We came home with the car absolutely loaded! The list, as far as I can remember, included one pear tree (variety unknown), three plum trees — one Victoria, a greengage and the other a Czar plum — five apple trees (both cooking and dessert), a flowering weeping cheery, an almond tree, prunus, malus, red May, several spiraeas, two clematis and a pyracantha. There were a few more — what they were I can't remember.

It was November, the ground was hard and the weather extremely cold but valiantly we planted on and on. All survived with the exception of the pyracantha. I couldn't really blame it, for our fingers were too cold to undo the string which held the sacking wrapped around the roots in place. Rob and I thought, optimistically, the roots would find their own way through — however, they proved us wrong! My dear husband muttered that he felt like a so and so mole, and by this time my enthusiasm was waning too.

In the two years we were there we built up a lovely collection of plants — the rhododendrons and kalmias, which we had been unable to grow before, were a joy to behold. We made a winter corner, one that could be seen from the sitting room windows. In it we planted Prunus autumnalis, which has dainty blossom appearing spasmodically through out the Winter months, then there was Viburnum fragrans and a little witch hazel, Primula Wanda, lots of bulbs and two beautiful Ilex (a variegated one and a smooth leaved green one) as well as a couple of mahonias.

The borders we had dug were wide and curving. These were planted with climbing roses and also some old-fashioned shrub roses. Against the brick walls of the garage we grew an Albertine climbing rose and a Virginia creeper. Outside the bathroom was the old white rose that we had brought with us from "Little Orchard" — Frau Karl Druschki. I grew tree lupine from seed — there was plenty of colour.

The bungalow seemed very quiet. Life as I had known it at the cottage and "Little Orchard" was non-existent. I was alone all day — Rob was at the office, Fan was married and my dear Aunt, who had moved with us, was now sadly in a nursing home. There was no traffic, no passers-by for we were situated at the bottom of a cul-de-sac. Gradually I managed to adapt, and as time went by we became acquainted with our neighbours. Knowing them eased the loneliness.

110

After a time Rob and I both went down with flu and he was home all day for a week or so. I think he also felt isolated in the cul-de-sac, for shortly after he said, "Let's move, go back to the cottage." For a long time the cottage had remained empty and was a constant worry to us both. Something had to be done to save it from falling into a worse state of disrepair, and moving back there seemed to be the obvious solution. The bungalow was all very well but not for us! We advertised it — June passed, as did July, August and then we were into September. Towards the end of the month two would-be purchasers arrived and it was a race between them to see who sold their property first. In fact they both sold within a couple of days of each other and we could have sold our bungalow twice over!

Feverishly I began to pack. Boxes of all sizes and anything I could lay my hands on were filled. The furniture removers said I had been busy! They had never seen so many little boxes in their lives — and they had seen some! Soon the removal men had gone from the bungalow and we loaded up all the things we would need into our touring caravan (two berth and small), but more about that later! We then followed the rest of our worldly goods back to the cottage, which we felt had always waited for us to come back.

CHAPTER
TWENTY-FIVE

The view from my old bedroom window remained unchanged, I could still see the winding lane and, at its end, the church tower just visible. One of the first things I did, as soon as time allowed, was to retrace my steps along the lane to the Church, as I had on my wedding day and when Fan had been christened, but this time I was going to visit my loved ones who lie sleeping in that peaceful Churchyard. It is a Churchyard where snowdrops bloom and later, in the Spring, the grass is studded with primroses and in places white violets grow in profusion. Generations of my ancestors lay at rest there. Their lives had been lived in this village and the surrounding land had been farmed by them. I read again the names on the old headstones and wondered what joys and sorrows they had experienced, and as I read the names of those dear to me, whose lives I once shared, the memories came flooding back.

We had parked the caravan at the side of the cottage, as we intended to live in it for the time being until we had made the house habitable. The removal men had stacked the furniture and boxes in a couple of rooms. As usual there was plenty of work to be done and quickly too, if we were to be installed comfortably inside before the Winter weather was upon us. But first of all we felt we would work better if we took a short holiday.

The caravan we had bought optimistically for touring was rather small for comfort and there was not the same gay, light-hearted feeling we had experienced, when we had toured the New Forest some months earlier. How lovely it had been to walk in the Spring heather and watch the ponies grazing contentedly near the caravan. It had rained heavily, but that had not seemed important — it had been a lovely holiday. Take for instance the day we had gone to Ringwood market — what a rewarding time that had been — I had acquired 14 new plants! We enjoyed buying at the auction which was held in the Market square. Fruit, flowers, vegetables, plants, second-hand furniture, harness and a glorious miscellany were disposed of. All the World and his wife came from far and near for their weekly day out. "What do you want all those plants for?" Rob had asked good-naturally as he helped to pack them in the car. Each night he also helped me take them out of the caravan (so that we could get in) and carefully placed them under the van, where we hoped the ponies would not reach them! He had long resigned himself to my plant mania — perhaps there is something in the old adage "If you can't beat them, join them!"

But this time we were not going to the New Forest — we were going to Scarborough! It was October, what a delightful time to go North, breezy and bracing, I would say!

The field we had chosen, on the outskirts of Scarborough, only had one caravan in it which was parked in a hollow, close to the hedgerow, right at the bottom of the field. Gradually we towed our small caravan into the position we had chosen. Not exactly in the centre of the field, but almost, on top of a small hill. What a lovely view of Yorkshire we had. We could almost see, but not quite, Scalby Mills. Rob enthusiastically pointed out the landmarks of his beloved native county and from our lofty perch we surveyed the scenery as he relived the holidays he had spent in this area as a boy.

For two days and nights all was well, but on the third night the gales began, gently at first, then the caravan began to rock. Never daunted, I climbed into my bunk bed and prepared to be lulled to sleep. How cosy I was tucked up in my little sleeping bag, how thoughtful I had been to choose the one that didn't have the faulty zip! Rob had had trouble with that when he had fallen out of his bunk and could not get up because the sleeping bag would not unzip! However, not to be put off, Rob climbed into his bunk, but only for five minutes! The wind blew, but not so gently now. Indeed the side of the van smartly hit my rear as I lay in my bunk. Vainly I tried to compose myself for sleep — then Rob shuffled out of his bunk, extricated himself from his sleeping bag — he really had now at last got the knack of that zip, I thought admiringly! With haste he started dragging on his clothes!

114

"What are you doing?" I enquired.

"I'm not staying here!" panted my ever-loving, self-preservation to the fore! "I'm moving the van before it tips over!" And with that he flung another sweater over his pyjama jacket. I got dressed! It seemed the best thing to do at the time — the van, buffeted by the gale-force wind, was a frightening place to be. Thankfully we both stepped out into the darkness and onto solid ground again.

Rob, armed with a torch and jack, began to hitch the van to the car, but not before staggering out of the caravan with the portable toilet which in those days was an added amenity to caravan living! He placed the amenity carefully on the grass. After making sure everything was safe inside the van, we piled into the car and towed the van down the hill, to the shelter of the hedge, where our now not too distant neighbours slept peacefully on!

On such occasions as this — not that I can think of another — but in any dire emergency I like to think I am extremely helpful! Rob was safely unhitching the van, so would be fully occupied for a few minutes. During that time I thought I would nip smartly across the field, and on my return present Rob with a lovely surprise — the chemical loo! Have you ever tried to find one somewhere in the middle of a strange field on a pitch-black night in a howling gale? It was at this juncture I began to go off caravanning! After something of a search, an irate shout reached me, then the wind began again, then another shout again rudely interrupted by the wind! A small light began to weave and circle the field. Wonder what that is, I thought to myself, can it be a Yorkshire glowworm? It was my husband — frozen to the marrow, teeth chattering from the cold.

"Where did you go?" panted Rob.

"I'm looking for the loo." I said somewhat apologetically.

"I know just where I left it," said he with assurance and made a beeline for it. I never knew if he was more like a bloodhound or a homing pigeon! Lovingly clasping our amenity to his bosom he trotted back to the caravan. I followed, somewhat subdued.

We hadn't finished yet — first Rob had lost me, and then found me, next he had recovered the missing loo, and now we had lost the jack! He had put it down in the long grass so he could shine the little torch and search for me. Now we had to search for the jack! It just wasn't our night! We stamped on the grass and finally the jack was retrieved. Shivering, I held the torch and eventually Rob, the loo and I were in residence again!

In the morning the sun shone and all was calm.

CHAPTER
TWENTY-SIX

Back at the cottage again the caravan was somewhere clean to eat and sleep, but it was a bit cold in the mornings and everything seemed damp with condensation, reminding me of the Control Tower.

We knew that very soon we would have somehow to install ourselves indoors, but it was in a dreadful muddle, not helped by burst pipes in the kitchen so every drop of water had to be carried from a tap outside. We managed to make the two downstairs rooms into a sitting room and bedroom and they were fairly comfortable.

The launderette became a real social evening — we staggered in with our load of filthy washing (and filthy really did describe it), then as our clothes tumbled and whirled themselves clean and dry, we met the same people week after week. Some consumed fish and chips, others unloaded the baby's pram because they had brought their neighbour's laundry as well as their own. Soon they had set several machines in motion and settled down to watch the washing process. Dutiful husbands arrived, dumped their washing in the machine and departed for the nearest pub — evidently they had it organised to a fine art!

The garden at the cottage was a wilderness again and so, as we had at "Little Orchard", we fought our way through elder and brambles. This time it was not with a feeling of joy, but one of sadness when we came across a rose we had grown from a cutting, or maybe a shrub which had now grown past its strength.

Again, as if in a mirror, I could see the garden as it used to be. I could see a contented white dog lying close to the lilac tree in the warm sunshine, her faithful old eyes, so full of love, watching us wherever we went. I could see my Aunt's favourite plants and I could imagine her there by the French windows as we worked in the garden, but now she had gone to her last rest. Oh! I could see so many things that brought a lump to my throat, as my memory stretched back over the years.

At last the downstairs was habitable. Main drainage had now come to the village and with this installed and warm central heating, life became easier. Eight years had slipped by since we had left the cottage, but this time we intended staying there. I now knew it was home: I had had to go away to discover this it seemed.

During those years Fan and Albert (her husband) had decided to extend and convert a small stone cottage, which strangely enough was in the village where I had been born. Rob drew up the plans — he felt, I imagine, as if we were starting "Little Orchard" again! The cottage had to be completely gutted and an extension built on, which then gave a long spacious sitting room with a dining end, a good-sized kitchen and downstairs cloakroom. Upstairs there were three bedrooms and a bathroom. The garden was small —

tiered with stone retaining walls that Albert built. Fan very soon planted flowers and shrubs, so that it became an established garden quite quickly. It seemed strange that she should come to this village and that our two grandchildren played in the field my Father had farmed, for it is now the village playing-field — and in place of the old stone farmhouse where I was born stands a rather nice village hall!

Quite suddenly, on a Sunday which began like any other, Rob's and my way of life changed completely. Rob without any warning suffered a stroke — it is something I don't want to think about, let alone write. He was rushed to the intensive care unit of the local hospital and due to the wonderful care of the doctors and nursing staff, he made, thank God, a good recovery. Fan and Albert were so good and as always a tower of strength. But our way of life had now to be reviewed, Rob took early retirement at 59 and we had to think of somewhere that was easier to maintain than the cottage.

We had a stone barn which divided our two gardens. We decided to sell the house and the garden adjacent to it and convert the barn into a bungalow. It looked well on paper — we had taken measurements and Rob had drafted a plan. However the planning authority felt differently about it. Planning permission was refused, so we had to think again.

Often we visited Fan and enjoyed walking with her through the peaceful village she lived in. On our walks we noticed that the school, which had been unused for some years as the children were now bussed to school in a nearby village, was standing empty. I felt it had possibilities! It was a long stone building with large windows overlooking a large village green. Rob's view was not the same as mine — "Too close to the Churchyard." he said and that was that!

No one listened to poor old Mum — they had heard it all before! Rob, since his illness, badly wanted to live near our daughter and he liked the village. I did too, for after all it was the village in which I had been born and with which I had never lost touch having had maternal grandparents and an aunt living there, and now Fan and her family. It was almost a second home to me — I had even attended that very school, as my Mother had before me.

To prove my point I said, "Come and look at the back of the school." To prove Rob's point, he did and admitted he was wrong. In fact he was pleasantly surprised! We had walked along a tree-lined road which led to the Churchyard and entered through the gate and then another little gate, which led into the school playground. Before us was a grassy bank with a well-established Hornbeam tree in one corner, the bank sloping gradually down to the tarmac. There was a wide-open veranda at the rear of the school building (all 60 feet of it), the school had three classrooms with a cloakroom at either end, large windows and, at the end of the building, a large school bell hung! To the left of the main building was a block of seven toilets and to the right a flight of stone steps leading onto a hard-surfaced playground, complete with an ancient apple tree. There was also quite a good selection of shrubs, while bluebells — pink and white ones too — seemed to grow everywhere. Even Fan was impressed, she could see a future garden: I could too!

Rob, just like a man, was looking at more mundane things. "The building is in a good condition," he said, "I wonder if it will come up for sale?" He looked thoughtful, "I might be interested at a price." At a price was right. It did come on the market but someone else wanted it as well. We had done our homework and decided it would give us the accommodation we needed, so we were very keen to buy it. Two months passed, it was now November, but at last it was ours!

The view across the green had changed over the years. The avenue of trees still stood sentinel — they remain unchanged — but now houses had been built and a little cottage, which I remembered well, had been incorporated into a couple more cottages to make a fine single dwelling. My memories of the cottage across the green go back to school days, when I had been invited by a small girl to lunch. Hand in hand we crossed the green — we were about six years old at the time — and the meal, which I enjoyed, maybe from the sheer novelty of it, I don't know, was mashed potatoes, liberally seasoned with salt and pepper and with lots and lots of butter soaking into them. This was the first course — indeed it was the only one — but never had anything tasted more delicious. Perhaps it was all they could afford in those days, but I have never forgotten it!

Rob got down to drawing plans and I ordered fruit trees — five apple, four plum and a Prunus autumnalis, for I regretted having to leave the one at the bungalow

121

but even Rob had jibbed at having to move all six foot of it! It was now Summer — a long dry one — so the fruit trees would be delivered later in the year. This suited us well. As before, I dug up and put into black polythene containers my shrubs. Those that were too large for me to pot up had been dug up and trenched at the School. Four trailer loads were moved in this way. Cuttings I had taken mostly thrived and throughout the Summer drought I managed to keep everything alive by conserving the bath water; even cold tea and coffee dregs were all used to good effect!

Someone else, years before, had been a lover of shrubs. They had planted quite a lot of good species at the School. In front was a lovely orange berberis, four different spiraeas and a holly. At each end these were flanked by a mauve syringa. In the playground there was a mass of dogwood, and a sumach, which unfortunately was intertwined with convolvulus. There was a showy snowball tree (viburnum) at the side of the steps and on the other side a white lilac. We found a small old-fashioned shrub rose, a Dorothy Perkins rambler and a forsythia. We were off to a good start garden-wise! Primroses and wood anemones covered the ground at the front of the School. Ferns also grew there and of course there were the bluebells.

At last the school was ready — not finished but we could move into it comfortably. The cottage was sold and we had, for the very last time, bade farewell to somewhere I had called home on and off for 40 years. At the School, gone were the three classrooms, which had been divided by glass partitions. Gone, also, was the long veranda. Now we had a large sitting room, with exposed beams and an imposing stone fireplace — a spacious hall, so large in fact that at one time we were able to put the dining table in it! The veranda had been enclosed, part of it to make a long kitchen flanked by a utility room (converted from the boys' cloakroom), the rest of it making a small room with a large bow window. This room was originally going to be the dining-room. It was rather small but got lots of sun as it faced South, so we decided to make it into a little sitting room from where we could enjoy a view of the garden with the Church in the background.

From this room we watched as the birds demolished the fruit from our new trees. Every evening in the Summer a small hedgehog used the same route past the window, disappearing among the plants on the rockery. A small rabbit visited us at times — it particularly enjoyed the arabis!

To get back to describing the accommodation — two bedrooms were situated at the end of a corridor, with a door dividing the sleeping quarters from the rest of the rooms. The rooms were large, being governed by the position of the large windows. The girls' cloakroom was converted into a bathroom, which led off the bedroom corridor. Upstairs in the roof space we could have had as much accommodation again for it was a tall building!

It was such a happy five years that we enjoyed life at the School, having family around, sharing gardening chores at the weekends, enjoying sitting together in the garden — so many things to remember for which I am grateful — but it ended. On this particular Saturday Rob and I went to another furniture auction and life was as usual, but by Wednesday he had suffered a massive stroke and the end had come quickly.

CHAPTER
TWENTY-SEVEN

Picking up the pieces I felt that the School, 60 foot in length with the village green in front and the Churchyard behind, was rather isolated for me on my own. Fan suggested I should get a dog again, so one Saturday morning we visited a kennels where stray dogs were cared for until a new home could be found for them. There, with a nose pressed through the bars, was a little spotty dog, every rib in her body showed through her coat, for when she was found, she had been starved. She was a funny looking little thing with large paws, likely to grow into a big dog if she survived. She trotted back into her kennel and we walked on. The next dog was a fully grown spaniel that was house trained and that was it — there was not a great deal of choice, the spaniel was the sensible choice at my time of life, but . . .

"I don't know." I said to Fan.

Her advice was to think about it. We went into town and shopped, and all the time my thoughts were of the little spotty dog. She hadn't had much of a start in life and needed me. And I needed Nellie, as she became later. Back we went and she came out of her kennel to greet us — we took her home, complete with diet sheet. The kennels had fed her, to begin with with half a weetabix and she still needed careful feeding to build up her strength, but oh she was so greedy, she snatched at food, anything. But gradually she learnt that her meals would always be waiting for her. She settled down and became a greatly loved companion.

I realised I must drive a car again, I had never enjoyed driving, always leaving it to Rob unless I had to, as I did when he had the first stroke. Though as soon as he was well enough to drive again, I sat back and left it to him. After a few journeys with a companion, I took to the roads again — forgetting Fan had put a blanket under the car bonnet to protect the engine from the cold as the car was left out in the open. All went well, or so I thought, for a mile or so — then in the middle of nowhere, the car suddenly shuddered to a halt with a broken fan belt! Endless cars passed, the drivers didn't want to know! Eventually one did stop, the lady driver helped me push the car to the roadside and then took me to the nearest village, where I phoned a garage, who fixed a new belt, after removing the blanket! I returned home, if you could call it that. I rattled around in it. With just Nellie and I, it seemed so empty and I realised I had better put it on the market and move once again, to something more accessible to the shops and town where I would be more independent. No more the peace of rural walks and surroundings and the beauty of this lovely village.

The School sold quickly and I had only a few weeks to find somewhere. Again (the story of my life!) I potted up some of my favourite shrubs and plants, but

126

sadly the garden we had made from the School playground and loved still held so many plants that I had to leave behind. The fruit trees were just coming into bearing, but at least we had enjoyed them — I was lucky really to have so many good memories. I viewed bungalows with pocket-handkerchief gardens. Then a pre-war semi-detached house that had a long garden came on the market. It was more than generous for my needs — or so I thought — so I settled for that one.

Moving day came and Nellie disappeared — returning eventually from a visit to a pig farm, where she had rolled in the manure. All the bathing and brushing didn't make the odour go away. It lingered for days! The removal men came and got on with the job though when they picked up the large chest freezer, the bottom fell out! We abandoned it in the playground to await the refuse collection. Having loaded up the removal van, the men informed us they would stop for lunch and then meet us at the new house. All went well, we collected the keys from the estate agent, and then the car broke down in the busiest part of town. No way could we ring the removal men and let them know we had been delayed. Fortunately it was a minor fault, but by the time we reached the house, the small front garden had quite a lot of furniture neatly stacked in it!

Nellie and I settled down to a new way of life. We acquired a kitten (Smokey), and after a refresher course my driving improved, or at least my confidence did. One day each week, through out the season, I acted as a room steward at a National Trust property. That was a lifesaver for me, it gave me so much pleasure and interest. There were so many interesting people to meet and I learnt so much while I was there. There was the history of the house to talk of, and for me, who had known the house all my life, it was of special interest. It was a friendly place, and for eight or nine years I looked forward to the hours I spent there once or twice a week. Then, no longer driving and with a degree of deafness (when I could have confused anyone!), I decided it was time to finish. I still visit though and remember the happy times I spent there.

Getting back to the garden of my semi, I had half of it paved and a trellis put up to divide the lawn from the paved area. The garden also had a dilapidated green house and was surrounded by a high fence. How I missed the stone walls and still do! Smokey climbed the fence and at intervals would present me with practice golf balls from a neighbour's garden. However much they tried to hide them, Smokey found them and, holding one in her mouth, would appear over the fence and drop it outside the back door. Clearly a gift for me, which I returned a dozen times or so!

After a few months I moved yet again — the semi had been a temporary measure until the right thing came along, which was a bungalow on the edge of an estate in the same village, its minute front garden well-tended and the bungalow well-maintained. The March removal day was fine, crocuses were blooming in the bungalow garden and an ornamental cherry was bursting with blossom. A sensible move, I told myself, and that it has proved to be. It's a friendly village and so many friends, old and new, are in the same position as myself so we keep in touch every few days and loneliness does not rear its ugly head too often.

I missed my rural walks with Nellie, but at last found a lane which had fields at the end of it so each morning we enjoyed our exercise. I threw sticks, which usually I had to retrieve myself. Then one day I noticed Nellie was drinking a lot of water. The vet diagnosed diabetes — it was a terrible blow, for I loved my dog and wanted to save her. Some people advised that I have her put down while she was still enjoying life. Many times I have wondered if that would have been the best thing to do. I still do not know.

We had 15 months more together. She went to stay at the vet's while they stabilised the diabetes. The day Fan and I collected her, she bounded into the room so healthy and well and could not wait to get home. She pulled at the end of her lead all the way up the garden path and was clearly delighted to be on her own territory again. I can not speak too highly of the care, attention and patience the vets gave. I had come home with copious notes, insulin, syringes, needles and sticks with which to test her urine. How I was going to cope with all this I did not know, but it was up to me to keep Nellie alive.

People were kind and a good friend and neighbour helped me over the most difficult beginning. I practised injecting an orange and gradually had enough confidence to inject Nellie with her daily dose of insulin. It was a nerve-racking time. First of all I had to collect a urine sample from Nellie, then test it. The amount of insulin she had depended on the result of the test. Often it was difficult to get a sample — Nellie watched me watching her and would not do anything. In desperation I walked her down the lane armed with my little pot. Never mind who was around, I was ready to get it under Nellie as soon as she squatted. I had to carry it home carefully to test and then give her her injection. The heartbreaking part was to see Nellie always hungry, wanting her titbits and biscuits and not able to have them. Food was three tins of Chappie a day and nothing else. Twice she had diabetic attacks and I had to get honey into her quickly — that was when I wondered if I should have kept her.

The time came when she could go on no longer — her kidneys were weakening. I rang the vet and he came and, as I held my dog's dear head, he put her to sleep. It was all over — a loved companion gone. Her spirit went to pastures green, I hope. Smokey moped and missed her for sometime, for they had got on well together.

CHAPTER
TWENTY-EIGHT

Twelve years or so have gone by — the longest, almost, that I have been in one place. During that time Fan and my son-in-law bought a Chapel and in the course of time a very attractive home came into being. There were two large bedrooms, a bathroom, sitting room, dining-room, utility room and a large kitchen, also two pretty gardens, one at the front and the other behind the Chapel. The character of the exterior was unspoilt.

This was not the only move for Fan and Albert. Again the years passed and then they returned to the village where my Father's ancestors had lived from at least 1500. So now with Fan there the line remains unbroken.

This is how this came to happen. Two elderly cousins of mine had spent their life living in a farm house in the village. 78 years they had lived there, the youngest being born there, marrying and moving with her husband to one end of the house, while her sister and mother remained in the other half. Divided like this it gave accommodation to parent and daughter in one half and husband and wife in the other! Eventually there were only the two sisters left, one at each end of the house! 78 years had passed and it was time for them to move on. Their Father (my uncle) had, many years before, bought four cottages in the village for £50 each! Over the years he had sold three of them, but had kept one for his unmarried daughter. She always hoped to end her days there, so any fruit trees she bought were planted in the cottage garden. In time the house was modernised and then after all those years in the farmhouse the sisters moved, with a few of their possessions, to the cottage.

Sadly the younger one did not live very long after the move, but the other lived on for a few years, enjoying her garden, planting her vegetables, gathering her fruit and entertaining her many friends, for there was always a warm welcome for them. Then, at a great age, she passed away, leaving happy memories and a cottage and garden full of fruit trees and flowers to Fan. So once again Fan was back. It seems strange that we always return to the village of my Mother's or Father's ancestors.

The cottage was extended and a stone was incorporated into the building of the extension. The stone had been carved in 1850 by one of our family and bears his name and the date. The garden now boasts a pond and lawns where the little vegetable patch used to be — but the flowers still bloom and the fruit trees bear abundantly.

As for me, I don't know, I wonder what is next? I tell Fan it will be sheltered housing. She says no, you will come and live near me again. We shall see! I have come to the conclusion, nothing is permanent — only lent for a little while.

ISIS publish a wide range of books in large print, from fiction to biography. Any suggestions for books you would like to see in large print or audio are always welcome. Please send to the Editorial department at:

ISIS Publishing Ltd.
7 Centremead
Osney Mead
Oxford OX2 0ES
(01865) 250 333

A full list of titles is available free of charge from:
Ulverscroft large print books

(UK)
The Green
Bradgate Road, Anstey
Leicester LE7 7FU
Tel: (0116) 236 4325

(Australia)
P.O Box 953
Crows Nest
NSW 1585
Tel: (02) 9436 2622

(USA)
1881 Ridge Road
P.O Box 1230, West Seneca,
N.Y. 14224-1230
Tel: (716) 674 4270

(Canada)
P.O Box 80038
Burlington
Ontario L7L 6B1
Tel: (905) 637 8734

(New Zealand)
P.O Box 456
Feilding
Tel: (06) 323 6828

Details of **ISIS** complete and unabridged audio books are also available from these offices. Alternatively, contact your local library for details of their collection of **ISIS** large print and unabridged audio books.

ISIS publish a wide range of books in large print, from
fiction to biography. Any suggestions for books you would
like to see in large print or audio are always welcome. Please
send to the Editorial department at:

ISIS Publishing Ltd.,
7 Centremead
Osney Mead
Oxford OX2 0ES
(01865) 250333

A full list of titles is available free of charge from:

We now offer a full audio book service.

(UK)		(Australia)
The Green		DA Books
Bradgate Road, Anstey		Unit 3
Leicester LE7 7FU		NSW 2065
Tel: (0116) 236 4325		Tel: (02) 9436 2622

(USA)		(Canada)
1881 Ridge Road		P.O. Box 80038
P.O. Box 1230, West Seneca		Burlington
N.Y. 14224-1230		Ontario L7L 6B1
Tel: (716) 674 4270		Tel: (905) 637 8734

(New Zealand)
P.O. Box 456
Feilding
Tel: (06) 323 6828

Details of ISIS complete and unabridged audio books
are also available from ISIS. Alternatively, contact
your local library for details on their collection of ISIS
large print and unabridged audio books.